THE
SIOUX CHEF'S
INDIGENOUS KITCHEN

THE
SIOUX CHEF'S
INDIGENOUS KITCHEN

SEAN SHERMAN
WITH BETH DOOLEY

University of Minnesota Press

Minneapolis

London

For more information on the Sioux Chef and our work in bringing Native American cuisine to today's world, please visit us at www.sioux-chef.com.

Published by the University of Minnesota Press
111 Third Avenue South, Suite 290
Minneapolis, MN 55401-2520
http://www.upress.umn.edu

A Cataloging-in-Publication record for this book is available from the Library of Congress.

ISBN 978-0-8166-9979-7 (hc)

Printed in Canada on acid-free paper

The University of Minnesota is an equal-opportunity educator and employer.

23 22 21 20 19 18 17   10 9 8 7 6 5 4 3 2 1

This book is dedicated to our ancestors and all indigenous people who have suffered through centuries of colonialism. We, the First Nation descendants, are living proof of courage and resilience. We offer our work to the next generation so that they may carry the flame of knowledge and keep alive our traditions, our foods, and our medicines for generations to come. We devote these pages to the earth, Turtle Island, our home, our everything, in hopes that we indigenous people will always stand strong to protect her.

CONTENTS

INTRODUCTION

It is hard to describe the era and the area I was born into—Pine Ridge Reservation, 1974—wide-open prairies, scents of white sage, bergamot, tall grasses, big skies, and dry, windy, dusty heat. You can smell the weather coming on from miles away. Growing up on Pine Ridge in the 1970s was what most Americans experienced in the 1950s. No seat belts for kids: we rode in the open back of pickup trucks with gun racks in the rear windows.

My younger sister and I lived on our grandparents' ranch with cousins a mile down the hill. We all were a motley and feral group of kids, as wild as the dogs we ran with, exploring the grasslands and sand hills, scouting out antelope, mule deer, pheasants, grouse, sandhill cranes, salamanders, mallards, geese, jackrabbits, bull snakes, rattlesnakes, prairie dogs, coyotes, porcupines. Our TV had just three channels, so, except for the Saturday cartoons or reruns of *The Brady Bunch, Petticoat Junction,* and *Little House on the Praire,* we were never tempted to watch.

I remember my father trying to teach me to drive a stick in his '76 Ford truck when I was just barely tall enough to stand up over the steering wheel. By age seven, I'd learned to handle a rifle and was good at hunting game birds and sometimes antelope and deer, could help dig the wild turnip of the prairie, timpsula, and gather chokecherries. We all pitched in with chores like mending fences, moving cattle to pasture, checking water tanks and windmills, tracking the horses and cattle. We were dusty and gritty, but I never knew that we were dirt poor.

Sean and cousin Justin on Pine Ridge, 1982

The family ranch was about twenty miles outside the town of Pine Ridge and about ten miles away from Batesland, South Dakota, population 200, where I went to grade school in a class of about twelve. Being members of the Oglala Lakota, we attended powwows, Sun Dances, family gatherings, holiday parades, school events. Native American spirit was always present, as was the strong sense of our family. Lakota-language class was as much a part of our school curriculum as English, social studies, and math. My grandparents were both fluent in Lakota, and people from the smaller villages would stop by to visit and talk for hours in that musical language. We were proud of our tribe, proud of our heritage.

Every birthday, wedding, naming ceremony, cattle-branding day, national and traditional holiday, our extended family gathered on the ranch. Our mom, aunts, grandma, and older girl cousins bustled in the tiny kitchen cooking up hearty taniga, a traditional Lakota soup, and earthy timpsula (wild prairie turnip), and Wojape, the Lakota berry soup. It's my favorite dish, and today, as it simmers in our indigenous kitchen, the warm, sweet aroma time warps me back to my freewheeling six-year-old self.

Except for the occasional trip to see other family and shop at the one grocery store in Pine Ridge, we hardly ever left the ranch. Our freezer was stocked with the ranch's beef and the game we'd bagged. Our shelves were lined with government-issued canned corn, canned carrots, canned peas, canned salmon, chipped beef, saltines, white flour, and bricks of bright orange commodity cheese. Although my grandmother tended a little garden, her fresh vegetables were a treat, not the norm.

* * *

I suppose it was my destiny to become a chef, but I couldn't have known that when my parents split up and our mom moved my little sister and me to Spearfish, South Dakota, to pursue her college degree. Spearfish is near a beautiful canyon, not far from the Needles Highway (named for the granite spires that jut out of the earth in the Black Hills) and close to our family's cabin. It's named ⬚e Sápa, in Lakota, and is close to Bear Butte, a sacred place for ceremonies and origin stories, considered the spiritual center of the universe.

For me, this hardscrabble city of 7,000 residents and 11,000 university students was a big, tough place—conservative, Bible-thumping, and white. As a brown and skinny kid with a thick rez accent, I was in the minority for the first time in my life. After school, I'd bike over to the university library where my mom studied and I was free to rove three full stories of books, a beautiful thing. On the rez, I'd explored the buttes and sand hills and here, in the vast open library, I wandered the stacks and pulled volumes of history, geography, anthropology, and fiction off the shelves and got lost in the thrilling landscape of ideas.

My mom, a single parent going to school and working two jobs, just didn't have time to shop and cook, so she relied on my sister and me to put meals on the table. Because I knew my way around the kitchen, I got a job at the Sluice as soon as I turned thirteen. Named for the gold-mining chutes, the Sluice was a short-order, hectic joint; I bussed and washed dishes and helped prep. That next summer, I worked at Sylvan Lake resort as the youngest on staff. I was a quick study and hard worker and soon pulled up to the grill. Our crew, college-aged kids, bored with steak and potatoes, explored new items such as rattlesnake and beaver, which for me was a thrill. I knew then I loved this work.

Another summer, working for the Forest Service, I identified plants in the Black Hills, documenting their history and culinary and medicinal uses, made notes, and drew pictures in my journals. Coded in my Native DNA is a sense of their value as food—purslane, wild yarrow, mint, bee balm, cedar, maple—all the edibles that surround us and grow under our feet.

Like most young men in their early twenties, I was overly confident and seeking adventure, so I upped and moved to Minneapolis, hometown of Prince and the Replacements, and landed in the Uptown neighborhood. Chock-full of independent restaurants, coffee shops, and music venues, it was diverse and crowded and I no longer stood out. I became sous chef at Broder's Pasta Bar and learned from chef Michael Rostance how to run a highly organized, efficient kitchen, skim stocks, roll out pasta, and navigate the wines of Tuscany and Bordeaux.

Kitchen experience, research, trial and error, and persistence made up for my lack of formal training, and I climbed up the restaurant food chain. By age twenty-nine, I was an executive chef overseeing several corporate white-table establishments and natural food cafés. But the price for such early success was high. Under the weight of soul-crushing pressures, the long, long hours and late, late nights, my marriage began to fray. I was young, I was burned out. I was hopeful and curious. So I headed to Mexico and took a year off.

We landed in the tiny village of San Pancho, officially San Francisco, north of Puerto Vallarta in the state of Nayarit. Its sheer remoteness and thick jungle prevented permanent European colonization until the late nineteenth century and much of the indigenous foodways have remained intact. Bananas, coconuts, and mangos grew for anyone to pick; chickens ran through the streets, and the fishing was great. I woke to the daily scent of strong coffee, chilies roasting over an open fire, tortillas baking on a *comal*. Kids in tattered T-shirts ran barefoot through the cobblestone streets, roosters and dogs wandered through the town at their leisure, plumbing was a luxury in the one-room homes. But the food, the food was bountiful, crafted from tradition, cooked with care.

There, sitting on the beautiful wide-open, tourist-free beaches, I watched in curiosity the local vendors selling their handmade goods and jewelry. The women and children in traditional dress were Huicholes, and I was fascinated by how similar their artwork, mannerisms, and sense of humor were to my own. They had beautiful beadwork that reminded me of the geometric patterns I grew up with in Lakota country, the colorful and meaningful plants and animals reflecting stories and legends. In a sweat lodge, called a *temescal,* they practiced ceremony that sparked my own childhood memories of our indigenous spiritual practices. I was consulting with a local restaurant in a small boutique hotel that sought to reimagine its menu with an extreme local focus, highlighting flavors of the ocean and jungle, mostly vegetarian with some local seafood.

In an epiphany, I tasted how food weaves people together, connects families through generations, is a life force of identity and social structure. After seeing how the Huicholes held on to so much of their pre-European culture through artwork and food, I recognized that I wanted to know my own food heritage. What did my ancestors eat before the Europeans arrived on our lands? I saw North America as a whole, with vast and varied landscapes, ancient migrations of people and agriculture whose methods and techniques spread northward with the corn cultures. I saw the deep connections to nature, to the entire ecosystems of the indigenous groups. I yearned to understand all of the plants and all of their purposes. No longer did I see "weeds," but food and medicine. I began to appreciate the purpose of everything in our natural world, to respect the plants and animals, sources of sustenance. As I began my research, I realized how grossly underrepresented Native American foods are in the United States. Mitsitam Café in the National Museum of the American Indian in Washington, D.C., was the only Native restaurant I could find. No place showcased the indigenous foods of our different regions; there were no recipes with dishes that featured the wild flavors of the landscapes (local game, heirloom vegetables, foraged foods) cooked over wood fires.

I started reading everything I could get my hands on and had books shipped directly to me—cookbooks, magazines, research publications—that covered Native American cooking, history, wild foraging, ethnobotany, anything that might provide a glimpse into our authentic culture. I was excited to get back to the States and start talking to elders and exploring our landscapes. I had a clear vision of what to do next.

In my mind's eye, I could see that long ago the tribes were sovereign over their food systems, maintaining food security through a rich knowledge of the land and its food resources. They cultivated crops, foraged wild foods, hunted, and fished as good stewards. They relied on complex trade, held feasting ceremonies, and harvested food in common sites. In order to understand this cuisine, I had to return to its beginning and work solely with indigenous ingredients using simple tools and basic techniques. I found that, more than anything, my ancestors' work was guided by respect for the food they enjoyed. Nothing was ever wasted; every bit was put to use. This sparked creativity as well as resilience and independence. Above all else, they were healthy and self-reliant.

Most of what passes for Native American fare today—fry bread or Indian tacos—is not authentic at all. My early ancestors didn't eat the foods I grew up with or cooked in restaurants. Other than the taniga (a soup/stew of bison offal), timpsula (wild turnip), bison, and Wojape (chokecherry sauce), I knew little about our food culture. The vision I had was all-consuming and it drove me to learn more in order to discover what exactly makes up an indigenous food system and how I could apply that wisdom in my own contemporary kitchen.

I moved back to the States, settling in Red Lodge, Montana, and spent a summer on the Lazy El Ranch, cooking, being outdoors, reading books, gardening, foraging, and planning. My vision became real in 2014 when, back in Minneapolis, I founded The Sioux Chef, a pure leap of faith. That August, I left my chef's salary, determined to focus on indigenous cuisine. By the end of September, I was hosting pop-up dinners, catering events, teaching and lecturing, building a team—all covered by our local and national press.

The Sioux Chef is a mission-driven enterprise of indigenous team members. It includes a full-service catering company, the Tatanka Food Truck, and (soon) a restaurant. We host pop-up dinners that weave together multicourse dinners with indigenous music, spoken word poetry, and

FOUNDATIONS OF AN INDIGENOUS FOOD SYSTEM MODEL

NĀTIFS
NORTH AMERICAN TRADITIONAL INDIGENOUS FOOD SYSTEMS*

UNDERSTANDING THE FOUNDATIONS OF INDIGENOUS FOODS SYSTEMS:

1
REMOVAL OF COLONIZED THOUGHT

2
RECONNECT SPIRITUALLY, MENTALLY, PHYSICALLY WITH THE NATURAL WORLD

3
UNDERSTAND AND BUILD INDIGENOUS FOUNDATIONS

4
REGAIN, RETAIN, SHARE, PRACTICE KNOWLEDGE

INDIGENOUS WISDOM

INDIGENOUS HISTORIES
LANGUAGES | STORIES/SONGS | PRESERVING
ARTISTRY | SPIRITUALITY/TRADITION
FERMENTATION | CRAFTING TECHNIQUES | HEALTH
FOOD PRESERVATION | SEASONAL LIFESTYLES
CULTURAL DIFFERENCES/COMMONALITIES | COOKING TECHNIQUES

PLANTS

FARMING
WILD FOOD
IDENTIFICATION
GATHERING
HARVESTING
WATER/ OCEAN PLANTS
SOIL MAINTENANCE
ANCESTRAL SEEDS
LICHEN / MOSS
TREE FOODS | NUTS
FRUITS | OILS
MEDICINALS

ANIMALS

LARGE ANIMALS
SMALLER ANIMALS
FOWL EGGS
OCEAN LIFE
FISHING TECHNIQUES
HUNTING
TRAPPING
BUTCHERING
ANIMAL FATS
INSECTS

ELEMENTS

PROTECTING NATURAL RESOURCES
FRESH WATER | SALT WATER | FIRE | POTTERY/CLAY
COOKING ROCKS | SUN DRYING | SALT GATHERING
OCEANOGRAPHY | KINFE MAKING
WIND DRYING | SNOW/ICE USAGE

The guiding model for all of our work at The Sioux Chef

storytelling. In my work with the Sioux Chef team, I also lecture, teach, and write about indigenous foods. Our success at local, national, and international levels confirms how necessary this effort truly is. We've shared our work in California, Milan, at the United Nations. At the Terra Madre, Shiilong, India, in 2015, a gathering of more than six hundred indigenous delegates, we realized that our work in mapping our own indigenous food systems applies throughout the world. Every day our work becomes richer and more interesting as we travel and meet with elders, indigenous chefs, historians, researchers, health professionals, and food justice advocates.

* * *

Why isn't the original indigenous diet all the rage today? It's hyperlocal, ultraseasonal, uber-healthy: no processed foods, no sugar, no wheat (or gluten), no dairy, no high-cholesterol animal products. It's naturally low glycemic, high protein, low salt, plant based with lots of grains, seeds, and nuts. Most of all, it's utterly delicious. It's what so many diets strive to be but fall short for lack of context. This is a diet that connects us all to nature and to each other in the most direct and profound ways.

This book is about the joy of indigenous cooking. It reveals the delight in finding ingredients right outside our kitchen doors. In a world that has become overcomplicated and reliant on appliances, gizmos, and tricky methods, we are returning to simple preparations that enhance the bold, fresh flavors of our local foods. These recipes, inspired by methods handed down through the ages, generation after generation, are integral to our culture, and, as with all good recipes, the dishes will change from cook to cook. These recipes are meant to be guidelines, not formulas.

We organized the chapters to reflect where ingredients are gathered with a mind to how most meals progress. We begin with lighter fare: salads, vegetable plates, soups, small plates that work as appetizers or starters or, when combined, make a full meal. The next chapter presents heartier dishes with entrées of fish, game, and one-pot meals. Next are stories and recipes for snacks, sweets, and refreshing teas to serve between or following those meals.

Our "Indigenous Pantry" chapter will guide you in stocking the staple ingredients. Many you may already have on your shelves or they can be easily found in stores, co-ops, and farmers markets. We also hope you'll want to try the less familiar wild flavors such as tamarack, cedar, juniper, and rose hips to expand your options.

We are not alone in this work. Our colleagues from other regions in the country have generously shared their knowledge, wisdom, and recipes. We often collaborate with these chefs to create indigenous dinners that reflect a diverse range of Native flavors.

Our final chapter, "Feasts of the Moon," illustrates our connection to nature's cycles with insights into our ceremonies and traditions. Here we create a calm, sacred place to celebrate Mother Earth's gifts, give thanks for such unrequited bounty, and honor friendship and community. These are also a guide to how we organize our feasts.

These recipes along with the stories of goodness and resilience are told with hope and joy. *Pilamaye* and *Miigwech* (thank you in Lakota and Ojibwe). Now, let's dig in.

HOW TO USE THIS BOOK

I didn't learn to cook from recipes and have intentionally written these recipes to be open to your own interpretation. Please taste as you go; trust yourself and make substitutions based on what's in season and what is growing close to your kitchen. Some ingredients may be unfamiliar or difficult to find. My Web site www.sioux-chef.com updates the most current list of suppliers we work with.

STRAIGHTFORWARD TECHNIQUES AND SIMPLE TOOLS

There are no tricky techniques or difficult, intricate methods. No special tools. Everything you need, you probably already have:

- heavy skillet (cast iron is best)
- griddle
- 10" chef's knife
- cutting boards
- deep saucepan or stockpot
- food dehydrator (not necessary but very useful)
- immersion blender
- mortar and pestle
- smoker
- clay *comal* or cooking stone

Our modern conveniences replicate ancient methods, whether we're cooking on the stove or a grill instead of an open fire; using the oven to dehydrate food in lieu of the wind or sun; and relying on coffee grinders, food processors, and blenders to accomplish what used to be done with grinding stones, mortar and pestle, and ancient mills.

ESSENTIALS

We cover the staples in our chapter "The Indigenous Pantry" at the end of the book. We tried to focus on the authentic indigenous foods of our specific northern Midwestern region, but it's hard to be precise. So many ingredients, introduced centuries ago, are now fully integrated into our landscapes and grow wild here—dandelion, purslane, thistle, to name a few. By the time I began hunting, pheasants flew across the plains and stocked every home's freezer. We're not purists, but we do try to source our ingredients with an eye to authenticity and sustainability. Here's a glossary of our key ingredients.

Salt: The indigenous people harvested salt and used it for trade as well as seasoning food. In our region, they would follow the animals to the source of mineral salts that appeared near streams. Several marsh grasses drew salt from their habitat so their leaves had a "salty" flavor. These were harvested to add to a dish. In our recipes, please use coarse salt. **Sea salt is best.**

Smoked salt: This adds a subtle smokiness to a range of dishes. Find smoked salt in the spice aisle of most co-ops, grocery stores, and specialty shops. To make your own, see page 183.

Juniper: We rely on the peppery astringent notes of juniper to do the work of pepper in our food. It's easy to find in backyards and along the edges of playing fields and parks. Fresh or dried, it's best crushed before adding; note that the flavor is quite strong. **Substitute with pepper.**

Maple sugar: A little sweetness adds a nice balance to the earthy, piney flavors we rely on. Pure maple sugar is increasingly easy to find in grocery stores, co-ops, and farmers markets. **Substitute light brown sugar.**

Honey: There's little evidence that the first people made use of honey. But it's so delicious and a wonderful replacement to refined sugar. We need bees on our landscapes because these pollinators are essential to propagating native plants.

Sumac: The lemony notes of staghorn sumac spark any number of braised meats and vegetables. Staghorn sumac is far different from poison sumac and easy to identify. Staghorn sumac berries are a beautiful bright orange or red; the poisonous sumac's berries are white or green. You can find Staghorn sumac growing wild along roadsides and in backyards. Sumac is available in the spice aisle of many supermarkets, co-ops, and specialty stores. To harvest and process your own, see page 182. **Substitute lemon juice.**

Maple vinegar: Also known as sour sap, this is made from the last run of the maple sap in the spring. At the end of the season, the sap contains less sugar, and when set out it "sours" naturally. It's less acidic than most vinegars and makes a terrific salad dressing and seasoning for sauces, soups, stews, and pan-fried foods—anything that needs brightening up. **Substitute mild apple cider vinegar and a little maple syrup, to taste.**

Eggs: We rely on duck and quail eggs in our recipes. Their flavors are richer because the proportion of yolk to white is bigger, but they can be hard to come by. **Substitute a jumbo chicken egg for a duck egg and one large chicken egg for four to five quail eggs.**

Oils and fats: We use sunflower oil for everyday cooking and rely on the bolder flavors of hazelnut, walnut, and pumpkin seed oils for sauces and dressings. The fat rendered from duck and goose makes a delicious medium for panfrying and roasting.

Herbs and seasonings: We collect and dehydrate the region's wild flavors—cedar, wild ginger, ramps, mushrooms, bergamot, sage, and rose hips—and work with local indigenous farmers for ingredients such as corn shoots, sorrel, and micro-amaranth.

SHARED VALUES/DIFFERENT REGIONS

As I've traveled throughout the world, I've learned how strikingly similar the indigenous approach is in every region. This book focuses on the Minnesota and Dakota territories—home to the Dakota, Lakota, Ojibwe (Chippewa, Anishinaabe), Mandan, Hidasta, Arikara, and Ho-Chunk—and the ingredients are specific to this region. But what I've found is that the methods in this book work no matter the ingredients. This concept is expressed in the recipes and stories from the other indigenous chefs who have so generously contributed to this collection.

(NOT) FRY BREAD

I'm often asked why we don't have fry bread on the menu or offer a recipe for fry bread in this book. Fry bread is a simple food but also a difficult symbol linking generation with generation, connecting the present to the painful narrative of our history. It originated nearly 150 years ago when the U.S. government forced our ancestors from the homelands they farmed, foraged, and hunted, and the waters they fished. Displaced and moved to reservations, they lost control of their food and were made to rely on government-issued commodities—canned meat, white flour, sugar, and lard—all lacking nutritive value. Controlling food is a means of controlling power.

Fry bread represents perseverance and pain, ingenuity and resilience. "Frybread is the story of our survival," writes Sherman Alexie. Yet, fry bread contributes to high levels of diabetes and obesity that affect nearly one-half of the Native population living on reservations. The average piece of this fried white-flour dough (the size of the eight-inch paper plate it's served on) weighs in at 700 calories and contains 25 grams of fat. When you pile on the processed cheese and potted meats of an Indian taco, you've got a recipe for chronic illness and pain. "Frybread has killed more Indians than the federal government," sings the rock star Keith Secola. Here's the thing: obesity and tooth decay did *not* exist among the indigenous people of North America before colonial ingredients were introduced.

Let's update this story with real corn cakes that enfold braised bison or smoked duck, authentic Native food. They taste of the time when we, as a people, were healthy and strong, and of the promise that we can stand up to the foods that have destroyed our health, the forces that have compromised our culture. And our corn cakes are easier to make and far tastier than any fry bread.

FIELDS AND GARDENS

Think of August's sweet corn roasted over a fire to be crispy and succulent, of poached eggs on a bowl of soft cornmeal, of a hearty, rich black bean soup. Not one of these dishes is difficult or complex and they're made with ingredients found right outside our back door.

To build the indigenous kitchen, I began by turning my focus to the foods that have always been available here. I had to shuck off layers of European culture and get my hands on native greens, herbs, vegetables, eggs, fish, and game foods that have stood the test of centuries. I began working with simple, direct cooking methods and the hand tools of my ancestors, and I learned to see the world through indigenous eyes.

After my year in Mexico, I took a job on the Lazy El Ranch in Montana—1,400 acres of unobstructed plains, prairie, and forest in the foothills, and I worked with a wise elder, ironically named Julia Childs. We stocked the kitchen with foraged ingredients—cattails, timpsula, wild mint, sage, and bergamot—and we harvested native pole beans, squash, and corn from her enormous garden. Under the big western sky, I could feel what life might have been like before the cowboys arrived, how cattle destroyed the Natives' lands where they lived, foraged, and farmed, and how lumbering decimated the once diverse and verdant forest.

Back in Minneapolis, it was easy to see that the foods we ignore or rip out as weeds are among the most delicious, interesting, and nutritious. Wild greens such as dandelion, purslane, plantain, and lamb's ear grow like crazy in our backyard. Instead of eradicating them, use them in salads and to season soups and stews. The acorns that crunch under car wheels, if gathered right when they fall from the trees, can be transformed into delicious gluten-free flour. A wealth of wild hazelnuts, raspberries, strawberries, and chokecherries grow along highways, free for the picking.

Before the Europeans arrived, my ancestors knew how to protect their foraging areas and they cultivated a range of foods using methods we've dubbed permaculture. The women did the lion's share of the planting, harvesting, drying, and cooking. They took great care of the soil and responded to the forces of nature in ways that seem remarkably contemporary. Buffalo Bird Woman, a member of the Hidatsa tribe, rotated her crops, composted waste, used every bit of the plant, including ash for seasoning, an ingredient in many trendy restaurant kitchens.

The work of our ancestors guides today's Native farmers and producers—Dream of Wild Health, Hugo, Minnesota, cultivates an enormous heirloom seed collection; and Wozupi, the Mdwewakanton Dakota farm, cultivates organic vegetables and manages a heritage orchard, in Prior Lake, Minnesota. Both are making these valuable indigenous foods available once again to chefs and home cooks.

The recipes in this chapter for small plates and soups are straightforward, boldly seasoned, and unpretentious. Some of the ingredients—maple vinegar, sumac, tamarack, for example—may be unfamiliar, but they make terrific additions to our stock of everyday ingredients and help us appreciate the unique flavors of this particular landscape. We hope you'll give them a try.

ROASTED CORN WITH WILD GREENS PESTO

Wagmíza na Waťóťo yužápi
Serves 4 to 6

Roasted Corn

Corn, when it's just picked, is full of natural sugars that caramelize to perfection on the grill or in a hot oven. Nothing could be easier or more satisfying than freshly roasted sweet corn.

4 to 6 large ears fresh, sweet corn
Sunflower or hazelnut oil
2 to 3 tablespoons Wild Greens Pesto, page 24

Prepare a hot charcoal grill or preheat the broiler to high. Shuck the corn and rub lightly with the oil. Set the corn directly on the grill or under the broiler and roast, rolling the cobs occasionally, until all sides are nicely browned, being careful they don't burn, about 5 to 7 minutes' total cooking time. Serve with dollops of Wild Greens Pesto.

Chef's Note: 1 ear of corn will yield about 1 cup of corn kernels.
Save those corn cobs for Corn Stock, page 170.

THREE SISTERS SUMMERTIME SALAD WITH SMOKED TROUT

Blokétu Watȟótȟo Íčhičahiya
Serves 4 to 6

Three Sisters Summertime Salad with Smoked Trout

Together, the three "sisters" are a nutritional powerhouse. The corn's complex carbohydrates, the protein-rich beans, and the squash's vitamins make a complete meal. Corn nuts are tossed in for crunch, but sunflower and pepita seeds work equally well, too.

1 cup summer squash, cut into ¼-inch slices
1 tablespoon sunflower oil
2 ears Roasted Corn, page 13, kernels cut from cob
1 cup Cedar-Braised Beans, page 36
¼ cup Wojape Mint Sauce, page 15
Dandelion greens (plus mix of wild greens)
4 ounces smoked trout, cut into half-inch strips

Heat a griddle or large heavy skillet over high heat and sear the squash slices on both sides, about 3 minutes. Set aside. Turn the corn, beans, and summer squash into a large mixing bowl. Toss with just enough mint sauce to lightly coat and serve on a bed of the mixed greens. Lay the trout over the salad.

WOJAPE MINT SAUCE
Wóžapi nakúŋ Čheyáka Iyúltȟuŋ
Makes about ½ cup

This is terrific with bitter greens such as watercress, dandelion, or sorrel. Store in a covered container in the refrigerator for 3 to 5 days.

¼ cup Wojape, page 173
1 tablespoon maple vinegar, page 18
3 tablespoon sunflower oil
1 tablespoon maple syrup
Generous pinch salt
1 tablespoon chopped mint

Whisk all the ingredients together in a small bowl. Taste and adjust the seasonings.

LOCAVORES AND TRADE-A-VORES

"Native people weren't locavores; they were tradeavores. And that extended into their relationships with the Europeans after 1491." — Lois Ellen Frank

How did corn, originally cultivated in Mexico as far back as 8000 BC, make its way as far north as Canada? Trade. Today, we may be linked electronically, but centuries ago, Native American trade routes were vigorous and complex.

Evidence suggests that the corn we grow today traveled along trade routes whose hub was Cahokia, an ancient city that covered about six square miles. First settled around AD 600, Cahokia had an estimated population of forty thousand by the thirteenth century. Strategically located near the confluence of the Mississippi, Missouri, and Illinois rivers, Cahokia maintained links with communities as far-flung as the Great Lakes, the Gulf Coast, the Rockies, and the Atlantic Ocean. It traded copper, whelk shells, and flint (chert) used in hoes and other farming tools. It shared its methods of planting the three sisters (corn, beans, squash) as well as cooking and preserving food.

As I build our indigenous kitchen, I'm not overly intent on limiting our ingredients to this particular region. While it's important to know the foods that are closest to our kitchens, I'm curious about the foodways of other regions. But, it's important to understand them in their geographic and cultural context and to work with them respectfully.

SALAD OF GRIDDLED SQUASH, APPLES, WILD GREENS, AND TOASTED WALNUTS

Watȟókeča Íčhičahiya nakúŋ Čhaŋháŋpi Tiktíča Mniškúmna
Serves 4 to 6

A sweet–savory toss-up, this hearty salad makes great use of leftover roasted squash or pumpkin. Use any of the winter squash varieties.

1 small acorn or delicata squash, seeded, peeled, and sliced
    into pieces 1 inch long and ¼ inch thick
1 medium or 2 small apples, cored and cut into rounds
2 tablespoons sunflower oil
Salt to taste
1 teaspoon chopped sage leaves
6 to 8 cups mixed wild greens
¼ cup Maple Dressing, page 18
¼ cup dried cranberries
¼ cup toasted, chopped walnuts

Brush the squash and apple pieces with a little of the oil. Heat a skillet or griddle over medium-high heat and pan-roast the squash until nicely toasted on both sides and tender, about 5 to 10 minutes per side. Remove and set aside.

Toast the apple slices on each side until slightly browned, about 1 to 2 minutes per side. Remove and set aside.

Toss the greens, sage, and cranberries with the dressing and arrange on a serving platter or individual serving plates. Arrange the squash and apple over the greens and drizzle with a little more dressing as desired, and scatter the walnuts over all.

MAPLE DRESSING

Čaŋháŋpi Tiktíča Mniškúmna

Makes ¾ cup

This sweet-and-sour dressing was inspired by the traditional "sour sap," or fermented maple sap, traditionally used to season roasting meat.

¼ cup maple vinegar
⅓ cup sunflower oil
2 tablespoons maple syrup, or more to taste
Generous pinch powdered mustard or 1 teaspoon Dijon mustard
Salt to taste

Put all of the ingredients into a small jar and shake vigorously. Season to taste with the salt.

Chef's Note: Maple vinegar is fermented from the sap collected at the end of the maple season. Because it is lower in sugar, it is thinner and more difficult to boil into syrup. Left out, it becomes what Native Americans called "sour sap." Maple vinegar is available through specialty grocers and may be ordered online; substitute apple cider vinegar when maple vinegar is not available.

HOPNISS

Hopniss, aka ground nut or Indian potato, is a tuber from a bean plant that tastes like a cross between a russet potato, yucca, and a raw peanut. The entire plant is edible—beans, shoots, and the pretty flowers. It grows in damp places—stream banks, lowland, near ponds—and can be cultivated in gardens. The tubers of this perennial plant grow like a string of peanuts along the winding string of roots. It takes about two years for the tubers to mature, and they are small—about the size of a quarter.

Hopniss is denser than a potato, closer to yucca, and takes a little longer to cook. Like potatoes, they're delicious roasted, boiled for salads, or simmered until very tender and then mashed. They may be dried and ground into flour to thicken soups, sauces, and stews or made into flatbreads.

SPRING SALAD WITH TAMARACK HONEY DRIZZLE

Wétu Watȟótȟó Íčhičahiya nakúŋ Wičháyažipa Tȟúŋkče

Serves 4 to 6

Spring Salad with Tamarack Honey Drizzle

One late-spring evening near the shores of Lake Vermillion, in northern Minnesota, Tashia, Dana, and I set out to forage for a community dinner later that night. Right outside our doorstep the tamarack trees offered their beautiful little buds, so tender, sweet, and delicious. We harvested a full pail and then, walking back, discovered a big patch of hopniss nearby.

1 cup hopniss, scrubbed, or yucca cut into 1-inch chunks

2 tablespoons sunflower or nut oil

2 to 3 tablespoons Tamarack Honey Drizzle, page 20

1 cup shredded Dried Rabbit, page 115, or good-quality turkey or bison jerky

2 cups pea shoots or sliced snap peas

6 to 8 cups mixed wild greens

1 cup sunflower sprouts

¼ cup sunflower seeds

Put the hopniss into a pot and cover with cold water by 2 inches. Set over high heat, bring to a boil, reduce the flame, and simmer until tender, about 10 to 20 minutes. Drain and set aside.

　·　FIELDS AND GARDENS

In a small bowl, whisk together the oil and Tamarack Honey Drizzle. In a separate bowl, toss together the dried meat, pea shoots, and enough of the Tamarack Honey Drizzle–oil mixture to lightly coat. Arrange the greens on a large serving platter or individual plates. Arrange the meat and peas over the greens and drizzle with a little more of the Tamarack Honey Drizzle. Garnish with the sunflower sprouts and sunflower seeds.

Chef's Note: If using yucca instead of hopniss, peel the yucca, cut into chunks, and boil until tender, 5 to 10 minutes.

TAMARACK HONEY DRIZZLE
Wičháyažipa Tȟúŋkče Akáštaŋpi
Makes ½ cup

The tender spring shoots of the tamarack tree are nutritious, slightly sweet, and a little piney. We keep this drizzle on hand for brushing over game and vegetables and for sweetening tea.

½ cup honey
2 tablespoons tamarack shoots or fresh rosemary
Water as needed

In a small saucepan, warm the honey and tamarack shoots until baby-bottle temperature. Puree in a blender or food processor, adding a little water to thin as necessary. Transfer to a clean glass jar and store on the counter out of sunlight.

DEVILED DUCK EGGS

Maǧáksiča Wítka na Watȟótȟo yužápi nakúŋ Waȟčázi Čhamní

Serves 4 to 6

Deviled Duck Eggs

Duck eggs are bigger and far richer-tasting than chicken eggs. If they're not available, simply substitute 1 jumbo chicken egg for each duck egg in any given dish. This makes a terrific starter course or a nice, light lunch.

4 duck eggs
½ cup Duck Egg Aioli, page 23
Splash of maple syrup or more to taste
Pinch smoked salt
Pinch crushed juniper
Pinch sumac

Put the eggs into a large pot and cover with cold water by 3 inches. Set over a medium flame, bring to a boil, reduce the heat, and simmer for 8 minutes. Remove, drain, and run the eggs under cold water. Peel, slice in half, then remove the yolks to a food processor fitted with a steel blade. Add the remaining ingredients and process until very smooth. Adjust the seasoning. Spoon the yolk mixture back into the white halves.

- Find duck eggs at most natural food co-ops and farmers markets. You may substitute 1 jumbo chicken egg per 1 duck egg.
- Find smoked salt in the spice sections of most grocery stores, co-ops, specialty shops, and online. To make your own, see page 183.

DUCK EGG AIOLI

Maǧáksiča Wítka na Pšíŋkčeka Iyúltȟuŋ
Makes about 1½ cups

This homemade sauce has a velvety texture and rich flavor. It's a great foundation for the variety of sauces we use to dress grilled or roasted vegetables, daub on meats, and slather on savory cakes. Use apple cider vinegar if maple vinegar isn't available.

2 duck egg yolks, at room temperature
Pinch salt
Pinch sumac
Pinch crushed juniper
1 teaspoon dry mustard or 1 tablespoon Dijon mustard
1 to 1¼ cups sunflower oil
2 teaspoons maple vinegar

In a small bowl, whisk the egg yolk until thick and sticky; then whisk in the salt, sumac, mustard and juniper, and then slowly drip in the oil, a little at a time. Once the mix begins to thicken, whisk in the remaining oil in a slow, steady stream. Then whisk in the maple vinegar. Season to taste with the juniper.

Duck Egg Aioli

WILD GREENS PESTO

Watȟótȟo yužápi
Makes 1½ cups

To make a bold, flavorful pesto, I try to balance a range of flavors: fragrant mint, potent mustard, citrusy sorrel or purslane, bitter dandelion, neutral lamb's quarters. Making pesto the old-fashioned way by pounding together the greens, nuts, and oil will yield a thick, rough sauce.

If you'd like something smoother, blend it all together in a food processor fitted with a steel blade. This will keep a week or more in the refrigerator in a covered container.

Wood sorrel, like its domestic cousin, adds a bright, lemony flavor to this sauce.

2 cups wild greens, some combination of sorrel, dandelion greens,
**   purslane, lamb's quarters, wild mint, and mustard**
1 wild onion or ¼ cup chopped shallot
¼ cup toasted sunflower seeds*
⅔ to ¾ cup sunflower or hazelnut oil
Pinch salt
Pinch maple sugar

Pound together the greens, onion or shallot, and sunflower seeds with a mortar and pestle or by whizzing in a food processor fitted with a steel blade. Slowly work in the oil and season to taste with salt and a little maple sugar.

*To toast sunflower seeds, see page 158 or use unsalted toasted sunflower seeds, available in the bulk section of the co-op or packaged.

WILD GREENS

We've become so accustomed to ridding our gardens and lawns of dandelion greens, purslane, plantain, and other wild greens that we've forgotten they are good food. Although it's unclear if dandelions, purslane, and plantain are indigenous, there is some evidence that they may have reached North America in the pre-Columbian era, suggesting that these plants were already being eaten by Native Americans before Europeans arrived. Add wood sorrel, watercress, lamb's quarters, miner's lettuce, clover, and garlic mustard that grow wild in backyards, fields, and the borders of forests, and you have a great salad mix—delicious and loaded with vitamins. Instead of trying to eradicate these plants in our lawns, we can just eat them up!

Foraging for wild greens

WILD GREENS GLOSSARY

AMARANTH

The entire amaranth plant is edible—its tiny shoots, the green leaves, stems, seeds, and roots. When harvested young, they add zip to salads and pesto and make a lively garnish for soups.

CHICKWEED

Early in the season, the entire plant is still tender and bright tasting, so we use it all in salads and pesto. Early in the season the leaves are mild, succulent, and delicate, then they grow bitter as the months progress.

CLOVER

Clover is the first green to appear in the spring and tastiest when it's enjoyed early on. As the season progresses, it becomes bitter.

DANDELION

This is our favorite spring green—lively and peppery, great in salads and wonderful in pesto. We often chop it to garnish soups and light stews. The entire plant is edible, so don't hesitate to use the pretty yellow flowers for garnish; when they first bloom, their flavor is mild and almost sweet.

DOCK

The big spiky leaves taste a little like lemony spinach. As the season progresses, they can become very astringent but suitable chopped and used as a garnish.

KNOTWEED

The young greens and stems are great diced in salads; peppery and grassy, they add zip.

LAMB'S QUARTERS

Lamb's quarters absorbs minerals from the soil and can add a lovely salty flavor to salads or pesto. The leaves can also be used like spinach, lightly sautéed or added to soups and stews at the last minute.

MALLOW

Mallow is one of the last greens of the harvest and one of the first to return in the spring. It is mild tasting. The entire plant, when diced, helps thickens soups and stews.

MUSTARD

Mustard greens make a spicy addition to salads and pesto.
The seeds are easy to harvest for spice and homemade mustard.

PLANTAIN

Plantain leaves are delicious in salads, especially
in those tossed with berries and apples.

PURSLANE

This is one of the most nutritious greens on the planet—loaded with vitamins
and minerals. It contains more vitamin E than spinach, more beta-carotene
than carrots, and is 2.5 percent protein. It is chock-full of omega 3 fatty
acids that help boost the immune system and support brain function.

WATERCRESS

Watercress grows along fast-running cold streams and is one of the first
greens to appear through the crusts of snow. It's bright and peppery,
fabulous in salads, and great in pesto. It pairs perfectly with trout.

Foraging at dusk

STUFFED SQUASH BLOSSOMS
Wagmú Wanáȟča nakúŋ Wičháyažipa Tȟúŋkče Akáštaŋpi
Serves 4 to 6

Every gardener knows that late summer brings a bumper crop of zucchini and summer squash blossoms. These beautiful blossoms are far less delicate than they look. Try them stuffed with our Smoked Whitefish and White Bean Spread for an appetizer or light meal.

12 to 16 squash blossoms, stems removed
½ cup Smoked Whitefish and White Bean Spread, page 44
2 duck eggs, separated
½ cup masa or corn flour
½ cup sunflower oil
Tamarack Honey Drizzle, page 20, or honey

Lay the blossoms on a dry surface. Gently open each blossom and, using a tablespoon and your fingers, insert just enough of the spread to fill the blossom. Twist the blossom end to close and secure the filling.

In a medium bowl, whip the egg whites into stiff peaks. In a separate bowl, whip the egg yolks until pale. Gently fold the yolks into the whites, being careful not to deflate. Spread the flour onto a plate.

Pour the oil into a heavy skillet and set over medium-high heat. When the oil begins to ripple (and reaches 375°F), dip the blossoms into the egg mixture and roll in the flour to lightly coat and fry several at a time. Don't crowd the pan. Turn them gently until golden brown, about 3 to 5 minutes, and set on a paper towel to drain, while you fry the rest. You may hold the cooked blossoms in a low (250°F oven). To serve, drizzle lightly with Tamarack Honey Drizzle.

SAUTÉED CORN MUSHROOMS WITH FRESH CORN AND FRIED SAGE

Wagmíza na Wagmíza Aíčhaǧe na Phežíȟota Čheúŋpapi

Serves 4 to 6

This dish reminds me of the year I spent in Mexico, where corn is celebrated in all of its forms. Corn smut or maize mushrooms are considered a delicacy and it's no wonder. They impart a sweet, earthy corn flavor to soups, stews, and sautés and are especially delicious cooked with corn. This is delicious served over Corn Cakes, page 51, or Crispy Bean Cakes, page 38.

3 tablespoons sunflower oil

3 cups diced fresh mushrooms

1 cup corn mushrooms or dried, reconstituted wild mushrooms, such as chanterelles

¼ cup chopped wild onions or shallots

2 cups sweet corn kernels

1 cup soaked and cooked hominy, page 31

¼ cup Corn Stock, page 170, or mushroom soaking water

Pinch crushed juniper

2 teaspoons chopped sage

2 teaspoons chopped mint

Pinch salt

6 sage leaves

Film the skillet with 2 tablespoons of the oil and set over medium heat and sauté the fresh mushrooms with the corn mushrooms until very dark, about 5 to 7 minutes. Add the onions and continue cooking until the onion is translucent. Then add the corn kernels and hominy. Cook, stirring occasionally, until the fresh corn is just cooked and tender, about 5 minutes; then stir in the corn stock, chopped sage, and mint and cook until the liquid reduces by half. Season with salt and juniper to taste.

In a small skillet, heat the remaining oil over high flame and fry the sage leaves until dark and crisp, about 15 to 30 seconds per side.

Serve the corn hot or at room temperature topped with the fried sage leaves.

- If you know a corn farmer and can get your hands on fresh corn mushrooms, by all means use those in this dish. Otherwise, use frozen or canned and drained corn, mushrooms available in Mexican and specialty stores and online.

- To reconstitute wild mushrooms, simply cover with warm water and let sit until plump. Drain, reserving the soaking water, and squeeze out any excess moisture. Use as you would fresh mushrooms.

Chef's Note: To prepare hominy or dried corn, soak in water to cover overnight. Drain and turn into a pot and cover with water by 2 inches. Set over medium-high heat, bring to a boil, reduce the heat, and simmer until the kernels are tender, 10 to 25 minutes. Drain and proceed with the recipe.

CORN MUSHROOMS

Buffalo Bird Woman tells of gathering mape di, or "corn smut," or, to many of us, corn truffles. Parboiled and then dried while still on the cob, they were cooked with the corn. "We looked upon the mape di that grew on the corn ear as a kind of corn, because it was borne on the cob," she told her biographer, Gilbert Wilson.

Some farmers call this "devil's corn" but it's known as *huitlacoche,* or corn truffles or "black gold," in Mexico. The fungus lives in the soil and can bloom on fresh cobs just as they ripen. Gray and bulbous, the fungus can be lofted easily into the air and onto the corn plants, overtaking a field overnight.

As I traveled through Mexico, I found corn smut in markets and cooked it with poblano chilies to fill tacos and quesadillas and to toss into soups. In our region, corn smut was dried and used as a seasoning in soups and stews. Corn smut is high in the amino acid lysine and when combined with corn increases the protein content. But there's every reason to enjoy it fresh in a sauce or baked into corn breads.

The flavor of this corn mushroom is sweet, savory, and earthy, so, if you're lucky enough to know a corn farmer whose crop has been "hit," by all means use the fresh. Because it's so perishable, it's hard to find fresh, but it is available, canned or frozen, in most Mexican and specialty food stores.

BRAISED SUNFLOWERS (OR SUNCHOKES)

Waȟčázi/Pȟaŋǧí Lolóbyapi
Serves 4 to 6

We're familiar with toasted sunflower seeds and their valuable oil, but their gorgeous heads were also once an important source of food. The flavor is close to that of an artichoke. Once braised, they may be stuffed with wild rice, nuts, or beans, and they are also delicious served with a splash of Wojape or sprinkled with smoked salt. Serve these as a side dish or as a small plate for a starter or light meal.

If sunflowers are unavailable, Jerusalem artichokes (sunchokes) work equally well in this recipe.

2 to 4 sunflowers, depending on size*
2 to 3 tablespoons sunflower oil
¼ cup chopped wild onions or shallots
2 teaspoons chopped sage
Pinch smoked salt
¼ cup Corn Stock, page 170, or water
¼ cup roasted sunflower seeds for garnish
Wojape, page 173

Remove the flowers and the green petal-like leaves from the sunflowers to expose the pith of the flower head. Turn the flower's head on edge to trim off the yellow face of the flower, removing just the yellow and leaving the meat. Trim off the stem.

Film a deep pan or heavy pot with the oil and set over medium heat. Add the onions, sage, and a pinch of salt and sauté until the onions are soft. Add the heads with the "face" side down and sauté for about 5 minutes. Turn and spoon the onions on top, add the stock, cover the pot, lower the heat, and braise the heads until tender, about 40 minutes. Serve warm, seasoned with smoked salt or drizzle with Wojape. Garnish with the sunflower seeds.

*Substitute about 1 to 1½ pounds scrubbed sunchokes, sliced in half horizontally, for the sunflower heads.

GRIDDLED MAPLE SQUASH

Wagmú Čhaŋháŋpi Tiktíča Akáštaŋpi

Serves 4 to 6

Griddled Maple Squash

This simple technique for cooking squash is quick and easy. Serve the slices on salads, float them on top of soup, or stack them on corn, bean, and wild rice cakes

1 medium winter squash such as butternut or acorn, about 2 pounds
2 to 3 tablespoons sunflower oil
Coarse salt, page 183
Pinch sumac
6 fried sage leaves, page 29
Toasted squash, pumpkin, or sunflower seeds, page 158, for garnish

Cut the squash in half lengthwise. Remove the seeds and cut top to bottom into thin slices about ¼ inch thick. Brush the slices with the a little of the oil and sprinkle with the salt and sumac.

Heat a griddle or heavy skillet and lightly grease with the remaining oil. Griddle the squash slices until nicely browned, about 5 to 10 minutes per side. Sprinkle with the coarse salt. Then serve as

- a snack right off the griddle
- a base for bean cakes
- a garnish for soups and stews
- a garnish for salads

Chef's Note: To reserve the squash seeds to roast for a garnish, see page 158.

GETE OKOSOMIN— BIG OLD SQUASH

The Miami Indian tribe gifted seeds of an enormous orange squash to a Menominee tribal member, who saved and shared them with Mohican, Oneida, and Ojibwe gardeners. Winona LaDuke dubbed this ancient squash "Big Old Squash" (aka "Happy Traveling Seed Squash"), thought to date back one thousand years. Thanks to the care and thought of gardeners through generations, these seeds have survived through centuries of famine and warfare. Ancestors sewed these tiny precious seeds into their clothing while walking the Trail of Tears.

Drying squash slices on a spit, the Hidatsa tribe in North Dakota, circa 1916

LEXICON OF SQUASH

The squashes we now find in markets are descendants of this iconic indigenous food. Through the years, they've been hybridized with varieties from other regions and different parts of the world. Here's a guide to what you'll find and how best to use the different varieties:

KABOCHA

Nutty, earthy, and slightly sweet. Great with sage.

BUTTERNUT

Easy to handle, sweet, and delicious with mushrooms.

CARNIVAL, DELICATA, AND SWEET DUMPLING

Small, mellow, and sweet.

SUGAR PUMPKIN

Also known as pie pumpkin because it's naturally sweet and great for desserts and snacks.

SPAGHETTI

True to its name, it resembles spaghetti when cooked. Its flavor is neutral.

BLUE HUBBARD

An older variety, huge and silvery blue. Its dry, mild-tasting flesh is great roasted and tossed in a salad.

RED KURI

Smooth and round, chestnut flavor.

BUTTERCUP

Mild and dry-fleshed, well suited to savory dishes.

ACORN

An ancient variety, mild and terrific with wild greens.

CEDAR-BRAISED BEANS

Ȟaŋté Apé úŋ Omníča Lolóbyapi

Makes 2½ to 3 cups

Cedar-Braised Beans (Arikara, Hidatsa Shield, Black Turtle Beans)

Just a small branch of cedar adds flavor to these beans and helps to stimulate digestion and strengthen the immune system. We make up a big batch of these beans each week, then work them into a variety of dishes—appetizers, soups, and entrées. The first step is to soak the beans before cooking; it cuts the time in half. (This recipe is easily doubled or tripled.)

We like to use a mix of heirloom beans for a variety of colors, textures, and flavors. Because of the varied cooking times, we cook them separately and then combine them in a soup, hot dish, or salad before finishing the dish. Be sure to save the bean cooking water for a stock to use in soups and stews.

1 cup dried beans
3 cups cold water
1 5 to 6-inch branch cedar
Salt and freshly ground juniper to taste

Put the beans in a large pot or bowl, and cover with water by 3 inches. Allow to soak for at least six hours or overnight. Drain the beans and transfer to a medium saucepan or soup pot.

Add 3 cups of cold water to the pot and lay the cedar branch over the beans. Set the pot over high heat; bring to a boil. Cover and simmer until the beans are very soft. Begin tasting after about 25 minutes of simmering. Remove and discard the cedar. Drain and reserve the cooking liquid for soups and stews. Serve the beans or store in a covered container in the refrigerator for several days or freeze.

Chef's Note: For **Maple Beans:** Stir 1 to 2 tablespoons of maple syrup into the pot before removing the beans from the stove.

For **Mashed Beans:** Put the beans and a little of the cooking liquid into a large bowl. Using an immersion blender, food processor fitted with a steel blade, or blender, puree the beans to make a thick paste. Season with salt and ground juniper.

CRISPY BEAN CAKES

Omníča Ağúyapi Saksáka

Serves 4 to 6

Serve these as a first course on wild greens, or make them into tiny patties for finger food. They make wonderful appetizers and snacks.

2 cups cooked or canned beans, drained
1 to 2 teaspoons chopped sage
1 duck egg
¼ cup chopped wild onion or shallot
Pinch salt
Pinch crushed juniper
¼ cup corn flour plus a tablespoon for dusting the cakes as needed
3 to 4 tablespoons sunflower oil
Pinch sumac

Preheat the oven to 250°F. In a food processor fitted with a steel blade, pulse together all of the ingredients to make a rough dough. Using moistened hands, form the mixture into patties about ½ inch thick. Dust the patties with the flour and set aside.

Film a skillet with the oil, and set over medium heat. Working in batches, fry the patties until golden brown on each side, about 5 to 7 minutes per side. Transfer to a baking sheet and put in the oven to keep warm.

Beans

BEANS

Dried beans are the backbone of Native cuisine. High in protein, they add body and substance to soups, stews, and salads. When pureed, they become a soft dough for fritters, burgers, and croquettes. Here's a quick look at just a few of the different varieties.

ANAZAZI

Small, purple and white heirloom beans from
Mesa Verde, Colorado; quick cooking.

APPALOOSA

Small, spotted black and white, sometimes called Dalmatian; creamy.

ARIKARA YELLOW

Tan bean with a red eye, very creamy texture and mild flavor.

AZTEC

Large, white or purplish from New Mexico; very earthy.

BLACK TURTLE

With their meaty texture and distinct flavor,
these beans are perfect for hearty soups and stews.

GREAT NORTHERN

Larger than navy; creamy and tender.

HIDATSA SHIELD FIGURE

Named for the Hidatsa tribe and described in *Buffalo Bird Woman's Garden*. A beautiful pale-cream bean with gold saddle, this cooks up to be creamy and delicate.

JACOB'S CATTLE

American heirloom, kidney-shaped and cream-colored
with red splashes; delicate and mild tasting.

LIMA

Also known as butter beans, kidney-shaped and
great in succotash; very quick cooking.

MARROW

Small, round, and white that swell dramatically when cooked; creamy and mild.

NAVY

Small and white, they hold their shape when cooked.

PEAS

Split green and yellow peas cook quickly and are great for soup.

PINQUITO

Pinker pintos.

PINTO

Most popular in the Southwest.

RED AND BLACK NIGHTFALL

Heirloom beans with mild flavor.

RICE

Tiny, earthy, and quick cooking.

RIO ZAPE

From Rancho Gordo, brown and purple; meaty tasting.

RUNNER

Aztec, Giant Pinto, and others. Big beans that swell
to twice their size; need slow and careful cooking.

SNOWCAP

Kidney-shaped, pink with a white cap; sharp tasting.

SOLDIER

Old New England heirlooms, one of the original baked bean beans.

SOUTHERN PEAS

Black-eyed peas are most common. Mild and earthy.

TEPARY

Native to the Sonoran Desert of Arizona and Mexico, they're small and gray, white,
or brown; need a long cooking time, and their flavor is earthy and pronounced.

What about canned beans? Canned beans are convenient and can save the day in
a pinch. The best are natural foods brands such as Eden Foods.

THREE SISTERS MASH

Wagmíza na Omníča na Wagmú Patȟáŋpi
Serves 4 to 6

This easy side dish makes good use of leftovers; serve it with roast meat or fish; top it with a poached or fried egg for brunch.

1 to 2 tablespoons sunflower oil
1 wild onion or large shallot, chopped
1 small summer squash or zucchini, cut into 1-inch pieces
1 cup Cedar-Braised Beans, page 36
1 cup sweet corn kernels
½ cup cooked hominy, page 31
2 tablespoons maple syrup
2 teaspoons chopped sage
1 tablespoon chopped mint
Generous pinch smoked salt

Film a large skillet with the oil and set over medium heat. Cook the onion or shallot until tender, about 3 to 5 minutes. Add the squash and continue cooking until tender, stirring often, about 5 minutes. Stir in the beans, corn, and hominy and cook until the corn is bright and tender, about 5 minutes. Then stir in the maple syrup, sage, and mint. Season with the smoked salt. Serve warm or at room temperature.

Three Sisters Mash

SMOKED WHITEFISH AND WHITE BEAN SPREAD

Hoǧáŋ Ašótkaziyapi na Omníča Ská Iyúltȟuŋ
Makes 1½ cups

Smoked Whitefish and White Bean Spread, griddled smoked
whitefish skin, cooked black and navy beans, purslane

This creamy spread is great with our Amaranth Crackers, page 60, or piled high on Corn Cakes, page 51, or Wild Rice Cakes, page 63. This is the filling for Stuffed Squash Blossoms, page 28.

1 cup shredded smoked whitefish or trout
½ cup Cedar-Braised Beans, page 36
2 tablespoons sunflower oil
Pinch sumac
Pinch maple sugar

Put the whitefish, beans, and oil into a food processor fitted with a steel blade and pulse to create a rough, thick consistency. Season to taste with the sumac and maple sugar.

SUNCHOKES

Sunchokes are a quirky New World root that Native Americans introduced to the Spanish explorers who brought them to Europe, where they have been cultivated and celebrated ever since. They are sometimes called Jerusalem artichokes, but they are neither from Jerusalem nor are they artichokes. One explanation for the name is that the Puritans believed they'd landed in "New Jerusalem," and, finding the roots in great abundance, named them for the artichokes they believed grew in Jerusalem.

These roots, when roasted, become smooth and silky with a slightly nutty taste. They're delicious simply sautéed or steamed for a side dish too. Sunchokes are a snap to prepare. There's no reason to peel them; although the earth-toned skin is rough-looking and gnarly, it isn't tough. We just scrub them well under cold running water to remove any dirt and grit. Do not slice them ahead of cooking or they'll turn an unappealing gray.

Sunchokes "overwinter" well. When we harvest them in the fall, we always leave some in the fields through the winter until after the thaw so their starches sweeten a bit.

Griddled sunchoke

Raw sunchoke

MAPLE-SAGE ROASTED VEGETABLES

Phežíȟota na Čhaŋháŋpi Tiktíča úŋ Watȟótȟo Čheúŋpapi
Serves 4 to 6

Roasting vegetables draws out and evaporates their moisture, condensing and intensifying flavors and making the textures firmer and heartier. Use whatever is in season. Autumn squash is perfect for this, as are turnips or timpsula (prairie turnip) and sweet potatoes. These make a nice starter when garnished with toasted nuts and dried cranberries, or served over wild rice, on Corn Cakes, page 51, or on a bed of dark greens, drizzled with a little Wojape.

1 small winter squash, peeled, seeded, and cut into ½-inch chunks
½ pound sunchokes, cut into ½-inch chunks
1 medium sweet potato, cut into ½-inch chunks
½ pound turnips, cut into ½-inch chunks
2 tablespoons sunflower oil
Pinch coarse salt
2 teaspoons chopped sage
2 tablespoons maple syrup
2 tablespoons maple vinegar
1 teaspoon whole grain mustard

Preheat the oven to 425°F. Toss the vegetables with enough oil to generously coat. Spread out on a baking sheet so that they are not touching, and sprinkle with a little coarse salt and fresh sage. Roast, shaking the pan often until the vegetables are tender and begin to brown, about 30 to 40 minutes.

In a small bowl, mix together the maple syrup, maple vinegar, and mustard and brush over the roasted vegetables. Return to the oven and roast another 7 to 10 minutes to glaze. Remove and serve warm.

THE LANGUAGE OF CORN

"Corn is a common thread among Indigenous tribes throughout the Americas." — Chef Lois Ellen Frank, Red Mesa Cuisine, Santa Fe, New Mexico

Drying corn near Kenora, Ontario, in 1913

My grandmother didn't plant corn in the tiny plot she managed on the ranch. It wasn't until I landed in Minneapolis that I understood why everyone goes crazy for sweet corn in the summer. But behind this seasonal romance, is the story of how corn created the robust cultures of North, Central, and South America. The first farmers unlocked the mystery of cultivation, and corn fed populations of people in one place (Lois Ellen Frank, *Foods of the Southwest Indian Nations*). No longer did they need to leave home to hunt, trap, fish, and gather food; once they cultivated corn, they had time to pursue art, history, and science. Corn was a miracle—a highly adaptive plant that is easy to dry, store, and trade.

SWEET CORN
Grown to be eaten fresh right off the cob, lightly cooked, grilled or roasted. It's sweet and tender. It's also great dried and added to soups and stews.

FLINT CORN
Named for the hard, protective layer covering the soft endosperm with a lower starch content than the dent or flour corn. Often called "Indian corn," its colors range from white and yellow to multicolor red. It makes the best popcorn.

FLOUR CORN

Mandan Bride, an organic thought to have been developed by the
Mandan Indians of North Dakota, is once again being planted for grinding. Its
jewel-toned and striped kernels yield a multicolored cornmeal with a fresh, corn-
on-the-cob flavor that cooks up into a fragrant polenta and makes a tasty
cornbread. Growers today store the corn by shucking and then drying
the corn on racks before storing it in dry, cool sheds.
The cobs are then shelled before the kernels are ground.

DRIED CORN

Although any corn can be dried for storage or ground into flour or
cornmeal, flour or dent corn is preferred. Its covering is tender and it
will plump up quickly in a soup or stew without extensive soaking.
This corn makes softer flour than flour ground from flint corn.

HOMINY AND POZOLE

This Native American staple relies on the process of nixtamalization
that removes the tough skin from dried flint corn to produce a softer kernel.
The technique originated some 3,500 years ago in ancient Mesoamerica
(Mexico and Central America) and spread with the corn culture north
through North America to Canada and south through South America.
Nixtamal is known as "hominy" in the United States, and when ground
becomes "grits." In Mexico, the term refers to both the corn and a hearty,
spicy corn soup. When hominy is ground, it becomes a moist flour or *masa*.

Nixtamalization involves simmering dried corn kernels in an alkaline solution of water and wood ash for several hours until the kernels are tender. The kernels are then rinsed and dried for storage or to be ground. When hominy is ground into a fine powder or flour, it makes a soft dough for griddled flatbreads such as tortillas.

Ground corn

It's amazing that the first peoples understood the benefits of nixtamalization. The process increases the bioavailability of corn's protein and niacin and radically reduces the toxins often found in moldy corn. It also helps prevent the corn from sprouting. Ironically, the nixtamalization process did not accompany the grain to Europe and beyond, because the Europeans were already milling and hulling grain mechanically. But without nixtamalization, corn is much less nutritious and malnutrition struck in many areas where it became a dominant food crop. In the nineteenth century, pellagra epidemics were recorded in France, Italy, and Egypt and kwashiorkor hit parts of Africa, too. But thanks to nixtamalization, the indigenous peoples of North and South America did not suffer from any of these illnesses. In fact, they were remarkably healthy and strong.

Mixing corn and ash

SIMPLE CORN CAKES WITH ASSORTED TOPPINGS

Wagmíza Ağúyabskuyela

Serves 4 to 6

When we were designing the menu for the Tatanka Truck, we wanted something lighthearted, unpretentious, healthy, and fun. So, we re-created the Indian taco with authentic ingredients— the indigenous taco. The base is a griddled corn cake, like a griddled polenta cake, topped with local foods such as walleye, smoked turkey, cedar-braised bison, and roasted squash. This Simple Corn Cake is made of cornmeal, cooled, formed into a patty, cooked on a hot flat surface—flat rocks, a home griddle—just as many Native communities have been doing for centuries.

The variations on these easy, simple cakes are endless. Stir in fresh corn, herbs, dried meat, berries, maple, seeds, nuts, and mushrooms. The base of cooked cornmeal may be stored in the refrigerator for at least a week, ready to shape into cakes for breakfast, lunch, appetizers, and snacks.

3 cups water
Generous pinch salt
1 cup polenta or coarse cornmeal
1 to 2 tablespoons sunflower or nut oil

In a large pot set over high heat, bring the water to a boil and whisk in the cornmeal in a slow, steady stream. Continue stirring to be sure there are no lumps. Reduce the heat and simmer, stirring occasionally, until the mixture is thick and the flavor is rich and corny, about 30 to 40 minutes. Set aside until cool enough to handle.

Shape the cooked cornmeal into patties, about 4 inches round by an inch thick. Film a skillet with the oil and set over medium-high heat. Sear the patties until nicely browned on one side, about 5 to 10 minutes, then flip and sear the other side, making sure they are cooked through. Place on a baking sheet and keep in a warm oven until ready to serve with the one or more of the following toppings:

- Wild Greens Pesto, page 24
- Cedar-Braised Bison, page 120
- Smoked Whitefish or Trout, page 89
- Dried Rabbit, page 115

Corn cakes with a variety of ingredients

- Maple–Sage Roasted Vegetables, page 46
- Raspberry–Rose-Hip Sauce, page, 142
- Smoked Turkey, page 110
- Smoked Whitefish and White Bean Spread, page 44
- Wojape, page 173
- Puffed Wild Rice, page 175
- Griddled Maple Squash, page 33

BLUE CORN CAKE VARIATION

The ash from burning a little juniper turns the cornmeal a dark, indigo color and gives it a hauntingly smoky flavor. Simply mix ½ cup juniper ash with ½ cup water and reduce the amount of water in the Corn Cake recipe, page 51. (For more about culinary ash seasonings, see page 182.)

HOMINY CAKES

Pašláyapi Ağúyabskuyela

Serves 4–6

Hominy Cakes with dried apple and smoked meat

We sometimes make corn cakes with hominy instead of cornmeal. Because it's been nixtamalized, it has a slightly different flavor associated with corn tortillas. These cakes make great use of leftover hominy corn or cornmeal mush.

To make these, simply use leftover cornmeal mush or Southern grits instead of the cornmeal.

They are delicious topped with shredded Smoked Duck or Pheasant (page 106) and Wojape (page 173).

TEOSINTE

Teosinte, a grass native to Mexico and Central America, is the ancient ancestor to the plump golden cobs of corn we enjoy today. The skinny ears of teosinte sport just a dozen kernels that resemble rice and are wrapped inside a hard casing. Originating in the tropical Central Balsas River Valley of southern Mexico, the cradle of maize evolution, it's believed that the domestication of this wild grass into corn began about nine thousand years ago.

Just consider the capabilities of those ancient farmers. They were able to transform this wild grass into a high-yielding, easy-to-harvest food. The domestication process probably occurred in many stages as the plant was modified through selective breeding. These early indigenous people are to be credited with corn, which now provides about 21 percent of human nutrition across the globe. Civilization owes much to this plant and to the first people who cultivated it.

Teosinte is available to plant in gardens and may be found online through a variety of sources. We use it in the Sioux Chef's kitchen by toasting it first, then grinding it into flour to make crackers; to do so, follow the recipe for Amaranth Crackers, page 60.

Teosinte kernels

KNEEL DOWN BREAD

Čhaŋkpémakȟagle Aǧúyapi
Makes 12 breads

This recipe comes from Chef Brian Yazzie, a member of the Navajo Nation. We met as he was finishing cooking school at St. Paul Technical College, and he's an invaluable member of our team. Kneel Down Bread is a family tradition. Simple, nourishing, and beautiful, it's like a tamale but made with fresh field corn and traditionally cooked in an earth oven or over hot coals.

The name comes from the posture of Navajo women who used to kneel on the ground to grind the corn into a thick batter. It is traditionally baked in a wood-fired pit oven where corn husks are laid over red embers and then covered with clay to hold the heat as it bakes through the night.

In our kitchen, we rely on a food processor to grind the corn and bake the bread in a moderately hot oven. You can sense the generations of happy memories in this simple dish, a testament to the power of indigenous foods.

12 ears fresh or flint corn*
3 tablespoons sunflower oil
Pinch salt
Pinch crushed juniper

Husk the corn, reserving the husks for wrapping. Using a sharp knife, cut the kernels from the cob. Then, setting each cob in a large bowl, scrape down the cob with the dull side of a knife to release the corn milk into the bowl. Place the kernels and milk into a food processor fitted with a steel blade and grind into a mush. Add the oil, and if the dough is too stiff, add water, 1 tablespoon at a time, and process into a stiff dough.

Divide the mixture into twelve portions. Lay the husks rounded side down, then spoon the corn dough into each of the husks. Using strips of husks, tie both ends to enclose the filling. Gently fold the filled husk in half and tie the two ends together. Then tie another strip around the middle. Place on a baking sheet and bake until the package is firm to the touch, about 1 hour. Serve hot. These will store in the refrigerator up to five days. Reheat before serving.

*Fresh field corn can be sourced directly from organic farmers. If it's not available, use rehydrated dried field corn, available in many natural food co-ops or online.

SIOUX CHEF TAMALES
Wagmíza Čhoǧíŋ Opémnišpaŋ
Makes about 12

Often associated with Mexico, tamales are found in every corn-growing region throughout the Americas. We fill them with smoked game and fish, as well as braised bison and assorted beans. They freeze well, so make a few extra to have on hand.

12 to 16 dried corn husks*
1 cup masa or corn flour
½ to 1 cup water
3 tablespoons sunflower oil
2 cups shredded Cedar-Braised Bison, page 120, or Smoked Duck, page 106
Generous pinch dried bergamot or oregano

To soften the dried husks, place them in a bowl and cover with water. Place a plate on top to keep the husks submerged and let stand until soft, about 4 hours to one day.

In a medium bowl, beat together the corn flour, water, and oil to make a tender but firm dough.

Fill the bottom of a pot with a steamer insert and add about 2 inches of water to the pot. Line the bottom of the insert with a few of the softened corn husks. Open 2 large husks on a work surface and spread ¼ cup of dough in the center of each, leaving a 2- to 3-inch border at the narrow end of the husk. Spoon the shredded meat down the center of the dough. Fold up the narrow end of the husk. Tie the folded portion with a strip of husk, but leave the wide end of the tamale open. Stand the tamales in a steamer basket, open side up. Repeat, filling the husks.

Set the pot over high heat and bring the water to a boil. Reduce the heat to a simmer and steam the tamales until the dough is firm to the touch and separates easily from the husk, adding more water to the pot if necessary, about 45 minutes to an hour. Serve hot.

*Find corn husks at natural food co-ops, Mexican *mercados,* and specialty grocery stores.

OLD-FASHIONED CORNMEAL MUSH WITH POACHED EGGS

Wagmíza Yužápi na Wítka Lolóbyapi

Serves 4

This dish is especially soft and creamy, bright tasting, and corny. Top it with blueberries, fresh or dried, maple syrup, or even better, a poached duck egg. For this recipe, you'll want a heavy-bottomed saucepan and a sturdy whisk. Leftovers are fabulous made into cakes and fried.

1 cup cornmeal or grits
4 cups water
Pinch salt
4 duck eggs*

Put the cornmeal and water in a heavy-bottomed medium saucepan and set over medium heat. Bring to a simmer, whisking constantly, about 5 minutes. Reduce the heat to a simmer and cook, whisking occasionally as the mush thickens, about 40 to 45 more minutes. The mush should be thick enough to drop heavily from a spoon, but still fluid and not sludgy. Whisk in the salt. Remove from the heat. Serve in individual bowls topped with a poached egg or drizzle with maple syrup or honey.

*Duck eggs are ideal for this recipe, as their assertive flavor works beautifully with the creamy golden mush. But if they are not available, substitute free-range jumbo chicken eggs.

Chef's Note: To poach duck eggs, bring a small pan of water to a gentle simmer. Stir the simmering water vigorously to create a vortex, then carefully crack two of the duck eggs into the water. Poach for 2 to 3 minutes, or until the eggs are cooked to your liking, then carefully remove from the pan using a slotted spoon and set on the individual bowls of porridge. Repeat the process with the two remaining eggs. Serve immediately.

Old-Fashioned Cornmeal Mush with Poached Eggs

AMARANTH CRACKERS

Waȟpé Yatȟápi Iyéčheča Itká Aǧúyapi Sáka
Makes about 24 crackers

The only trick to making these crackers and cookies is to steep the grain long enough that it cooks into a good stiff dough. The dough will keep for several weeks, covered, in the refrigerator. Make a batch of dough in advance and then bake fresh crackers throughout the week. The longer they bake, the crisper they will become. A dehydrator works especially well for drying the crackers. They are light and crisp and gluten free. They make wonderful appetizers and are great for snacking and with soups and salads.

1 cup amaranth
3 cups water
Pinch salt
1 tablespoon sunflower oil

Cook the amaranth and water in a medium pot over a high flame. Bring to a boil, reduce the heat, and simmer until the amaranth becomes sticky and forms a thick dough. Stir in the sunflower oil and allow to cool.

Preheat the oven to 300°F. Line a baking sheet with parchment and lightly grease or use a silicone mat. Working with a teaspoon, put small mounds of the dough onto the prepared baking sheet and lightly flatten with your hands until they are as thin as possible, about ⅛ inch. Bake until firm, about 1 hour. Allow to cool thoroughly before removing from the mat.

Alternately, shape little patties with your hands as thin as possible and set on a food dehydrator. Dehydrate until very crisp.

AMARANTH

We see amaranth, with its purple-reddish leaves, growing everywhere—along the road, in abandoned fields, and across the plains. Sometimes called "pigweed," amaranth was first cultivated by the Aztecs more than eight thousand years ago and is now popular as a non-gluten, high-protein grain. We use the leaves for summer salads and sautés, and come fall, the grain, with its rich nutty flavor and high beta carotene, iron, and calcium content, becomes the base for our popular crackers and cookies.

Amaranth Crackers, Smoked Whitefish and White Bean Spread

WILD RICE CAKES

Psíŋ Aǧúyapi Sáka na Hoǧáŋwičhašašni Ašótkaziyapi nakúŋ Waȟpé Skúya Yužápi
Makes about 4 to 6 cakes

These are our go-to cakes for breakfast, as a snack, and as the base for a well-seasoned bison braise or duck. They're especially good topped with smoked fish and our bright lemony Sorrel Sauce, page 64. Make them tiny for an appetizer or big for dessert slathered in maple-berry sauce.

The recipe for these couldn't be simpler. It's just overcooked wild rice, pureed into a thick dough. We like to stir in a little cooked wild rice for texture. Once shaped, these will keep several days in the refrigerator, so feel free to make them ahead. Leftovers may be re-crisped in a low oven until warmed through.

2 cups cooked wild rice, page 81
About 3 cups water
Pinch salt
Generous pinch maple sugar
3 to 4 tablespoons sunflower oil or more as needed

Put 1½ cups cooked wild rice and water into a saucepan, reserving ½ cup. Place over high heat, bring to a boil, and reduce the heat to a simmer. Cook until the rice is very soft and the water has evaporated. Drain. In a food processor fitted with a steel blade, puree the rice into a sticky dough. Place the dough into a medium bowl and work in the salt, sugar, and the remaining cooked rice.

Scoop out a scant ¼ cup dough for each patty and shape to rounds about ½ inch thick. Heat the oil in a heavy skillet and brown the patties about 5 to 8 minutes per side until lightly browned. Transfer the patties to a baking sheet and place in a warm oven until ready to serve.

Wild Rice Cakes, Corn Cakes, roasted chestnuts, blackberry sauce

SORREL SAUCE

Waȟpé Skúya Yužápi

This bright, tart sauce is delicious on Wild Rice Cakes, page 63, Corn Cakes, page 51, or any grilled meats or pan-fried fish, or swirled into soup.

2 wild onions or shallots
2 tablespoons sunflower oil
4 cups chopped sorrel
Sumac to taste
Smoked salt to taste

In a food processor fitted with a steel blade, process the onions, oil, and sorrel. Season with the sumac and salt.

SUMMER'S VEGETABLE SOUP WITH WILD GREENS

Blokétu Watȟótȟo Waháŋpi

Serves 4 to 6

This is light and brothy the first day and becomes heartier a day or two later when the flavors marry and the starch in the vegetables breaks down to create a rich, thicker soup. The dandelion greens or watercress make a bright, peppery garnish.

1 tablespoon sunflower oil
2 teaspoons chopped sage
2 teaspoons chopped mint
¼ cup chopped wild onions or ramps
2 summer squash, cut into 2-inch pieces
2 cups sweet corn kernels
1 cup green beans, cut into 1-inch pieces
1 small sweet potato, cut into 1-inch chunks
6 to 8 cups Corn or Bean Stock, page 170, or more as needed
1 cup Cedar-Braised Beans, page 36
Salt to taste
1 cup chopped dandelion greens or watercress for garnish

Film a heavy pot with the oil and set over medium heat. Sauté the sage, mint, and onions until the onions are translucent. Add the squash, corn, green beans, and sweet potato along with the stock and simmer until the vegetables are tender, about 10 to 15 minutes. Stir in the beans and continue cooking until heated through. Add salt to taste and more herbs.

Serve garnished with the dandelion greens or watercress.

MISSOURI RIVER POZOLE
Mníšoše Makȟóčhe Pašláyapi Waháŋpi
Serves 4 to 6

This hearty soup showcases the indigenous Seneca White hominy corn from the White Earth reservation in northern Minnesota. This ancient heritage corn has twice the protein and half the calories of sweet corn and represents the strong tradition of healthy foods in our north country.

2 cups flint hominy, soaked overnight
1 small butternut squash, peeled, seeded, and cut into ½-inch chunks
1 tablespoon chopped sage
4 to 6 cups Corn Stock, page 170, or water
¼ cup masa or corn flour, mixed in ½ cup water
1 tablespoon maple syrup, or more to taste
Salt to taste
Puffed Wild Rice for garnish, page 175

In a large soup pot, combine the soaked hominy, squash, and sage and set over a medium-high flame. Bring to a boil, reduce the heat, and simmer, partially covered, until the squash is tender and the hominy is cooked, about 20 minutes. Slowly stir in the masa or corn flour, water mixture and continue simmering until the soup thickens. Season to taste with the maple syrup and salt. Serve garnished with the Puffed Wild Rice.

HEARTY MUSHROOM, SWEET POTATO, AND BEAN SOUP

Čhaŋnákpa na Bló Skúya na Omníča Waháŋpi
Serves 4 to 6

Hearty Mushroom, Sweet Potato, and Bean Soup

A warming soup that's hearty enough for a meal when served with Corn Cakes, page 51, or Wild Rice Cakes, page 63.

2 tablespoons sunflower oil
1 cup chopped wild onions or ramps
8 ounces fresh mushrooms, sliced
2 teaspoons chopped sage
2 cups cubed sweet potatoes, cut into ½-inch pieces
6 to 8 cups Corn or Duck Stock, page 170, or more if needed
1 cup Cedar-Braised Beans, page 36, or canned drained beans
Salt to taste
Pinch sumac to taste
Watercress or microgreens for garnish

In a large soup pot, heat the oil over medium heat and sauté the onions and mushrooms until the mushrooms have released their liquid and browned, about 10 minutes. Stir in the sage and sweet potatoes and stock. Bring to a boil, lower the heat, cover, and simmer until the sweet potatoes are tender, about 15 minutes. Add the beans. Season with salt and sumac to taste and continue cooking until heated through. Serve garnished with the greens.

For a dramatic presentation, arrange the soup components in the bowl, then add the stock. When serving, garnish with dried apple slices.

FISH HEAD AND WILD RICE SOUP

Hoğáŋ Pȟá na Psíŋ Waháŋpi
Serves 4 to 6

This soup could be made using a fish fillet, but you'd be missing the diversity of textures and flavors from the fish heads—dense, firm cheeks, the cartilage that enriches the soup's body, and the fatty eyeballs that add richness. We've added a little smoked fish to boost flavor.

Use any fish head you like, so long as it's big and meaty. The preparation is easy and relatively quick, and the resulting stock is fishy but not overwhelming so. Diners will understand pretty quickly how to pick the succulent bits from the heads, but if you'd prefer, you may remove the meat after it's cooked and serve it with the soup.

2 to 3 tablespoons sunflower oil or Rendered Duck Fat, page 105
½ cup chopped wild onions or leeks
1 tablespoon chopped sage
1 tablespoon chopped mint
3 to 4 freshwater fish heads (trout, walleye, northern, or whitefish)
2 tablespoons maple syrup, or more to taste
4 to 6 cups water
½ cup shredded smoked fish
1½ cups cooked wild rice
Salt
Sumac

In a large soup pot, heat the oil over medium heat and sauté the onions, sage, and mint until tender, about 5 minutes. Add the fish heads, maple syrup, and enough water to cover by about 3 inches. Bring to a boil; then reduce the heat to achieve avery low simmer and cook for about 35 minutes.

Stir in the wild rice and smoked fish and season to taste with more maple syrup, salt, and sumac and serve immediately.

WHITE BEAN AND WINTER SQUASH SOUP

Omníča Ská na Wagmú Waháŋpi

Serves 4 to 6

This soup works well with any variety of bean, or more than one. The squash cooks along with the beans so everything is ready at the same time.

1 tablespoon sunflower oil

½ cup wild onions or leeks

6 to 8 cups of Corn or Bean Stock, page 170

3 cups winter squash, cut into 1-inch cubes

1 very small sprig cedar

2 teaspoons chopped sage

2 cups Cedar-Braised Beans, page 36

1 cup cooked hominy, page 31

Salt to taste

Sumac to taste

8 fresh or Dried Apple Slices, page 177, for garnish

Film a heavy soup pot with the oil and set over medium heat. Sauté the onions until translucent, about 5 minutes. Add the stock, squash, and cedar and cook over very low heat until the squash is just tender. Add the sage, beans, and hominy, and season with salt and sumac. Continue cooking until heated through. Remove and discard the cedar before serving and garnish with the apple slices.

SMOKED TURKEY AND ACORN SOUP

Waglékšuŋ Ašótkaziyapi na Úta Waháŋpi

Serves 4 to 6

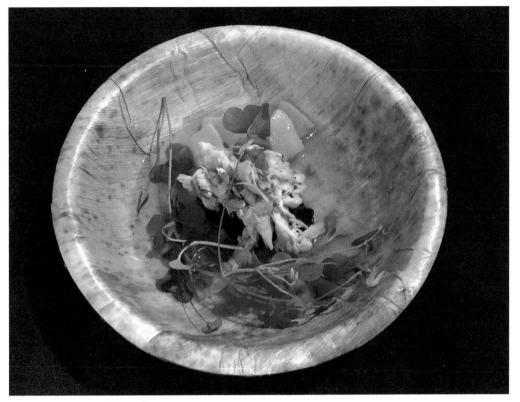

Smoked Turkey and Acorn Soup

The secret ingredient to this warming soup is the acorn flour. It adds a nutty flavor while thickening the broth. If this is not available, stir in the same quantity of hazelnut or corn flour.

2 to 3 smoked turkey legs
5 to 6 cups water
½ cup chopped ramps or leeks
½ cup Acorn Meal Flour, page 169, or corn flour
Maple sugar to taste
Salt to taste

Put the turkey legs into a large soup pot and add enough water to cover by about 2 inches. Set over high heat, bring to a boil, reduce the heat, and simmer until the meat is so tender it falls off the bones, about 20 to 30 minutes. Remove the turkey legs, pull off the meat, and discard the bones. Return the meat to the broth and add the ramps. Whisk in the flour and return to low heat. Simmer until the soup thickens. Season to taste with the maple sugar and salt.

SQUASH AND APPLE SOUP WITH FRESH CRANBERRY SAUCE

Wagmú na Ťhaspáŋ Waháŋpi nakúŋ Wathókeča T'áǧa Yužápi
Serves 4 to 6

This rich, flavorful soup has a creamy texture without cream. We use the small, tart crab apples that grow in backyards and along the borders of farm fields.

2 tablespoons sunflower oil
1 wild onion, chopped, or ¼ cup chopped shallot
2 pounds winter squash, seeded, peeled, and cut into 1-inch cubes
1 tart apple, cored and chopped
1 cup cider
3 cups Corn Stock, page 170, or vegetable stock
1 tablespoon maple syrup or more to taste
Salt to taste
Sumac to taste
Cranberry Sauce, page 108, or chopped fresh cranberries for garnish

Heat the oil in a deep, heavy saucepan over medium heat and sauté the onion, squash, and apple until the onion is translucent, about 5 minutes. Stir in the cider and stock, increase the heat, and bring to a boil. Reduce the heat and simmer until the squash is very tender, about 20 minutes. With an immersion blender or working in batches with a blender, puree the soup and return to the pot to warm. Season to taste with maple syrup, salt, and sumac. Serve with a dollop of Cranberry Sauce.

Squash and Apple Soup with Cranberry Sauce

BLACK BEAN AND YUCCA SOUP WITH WARMING SPICES

Omníča Sápa na Hupȟéstola Hutkȟáŋ Waháŋpi
Serves 4 to 5

Although yucca is associated with Mexico, several varieties can be found as far north as Canada, one of which produces agave nectar. Here we simmer chunks of starchy yucca and earthy black beans, spiced with a little hot chili, for a hearty, warming stew.

1 tablespoon sunflower oil

1 wild onion or leek, finely chopped

1 to 2 fresh chili peppers, seeds removed and chopped

2 cups peeled and diced yucca root

1 cup soaked hominy

6 to 8 cups Corn Stock, page 170, or vegetable stock

1 tablespoon chopped fresh oregano, or 1 teaspoon dried

1 cup cooked black beans or canned beans, drained

2 tablespoons agave nectar to taste

Smoked salt to taste

In a deep, heavy stock pot, heat the oil over medium and add the onion, peppers, and yucca. Cook, stirring constantly for about 5 to 8 minutes. Add the hominy, stock, and oregano. Increase the heat and bring to a boil; then reduce the heat to medium low and simmer for 10 to 15 minutes, until the yucca and hominy are tender. Stir in the black beans and season to taste with the agave nectar and smoked salt.

WOZUPI—AN INDIGENOUS FARM OF THE MDEWAKANTON TRIBE, MINNESOTA

We source nearly all of our ingredients from Native suppliers, a task that is becoming increasingly easy thanks to the work of Native Americans who are reclaiming our culinary culture. Wozupi, established in 2010 in the Mdewakanton community near Shakopee, Minnesota, harvests and sells an incredible array of America's oldest vegetables and fruit—Cherokee beans, Potawatomi lima, Oneida corn, Arikara yellow squash, Hidatsa shield beans, Lakota squash, *gete okosimin* (page 34), maple syrup and sugar, honey chokecherries, wild plums, apples, apricots, Juneberries, and crab apples. In addition, it offers its members Tribal Supported Agriculture (TSA) memberships to provide fresh, healthy, local food as well as gardening and cooking classes for kids.

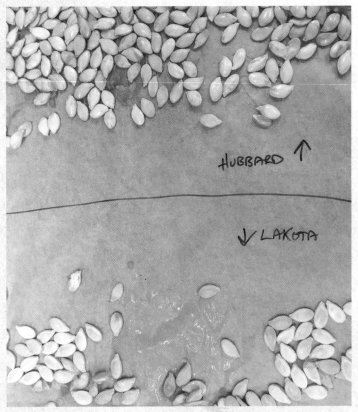

Lakota and Hubbard squash seeds

PRAIRIES AND LAKES

The day I turned seven, I got my first shotgun. It was a bright summer morning and I was sitting on the porch steps watching tractors bale alfalfa, a scent that's burned into my memories of summer. I was home alone that morning when my grandfather pulled up in his old pickup, a late-1970s Chevy Cheyenne that was well ranch-worn and smelled of prairie grass and manure. He would have been in his seventies by then. He and his siblings were some of the first generation of students to go through cultural "Reformation" on the Pine Ridge Reservation. They were forced to attend Christian school and cut their hair, and they were forbidden from speaking their own language. All of my grandparents were fluent in Lakota, their first language. My grandfather's father grew up on the plains with the Oglala, and when he was around eighteen years old he was in the Battle of the Little Bighorn (known as the Battle of the Greasy Grass by the Lakota). Shortly after that battle, and right after the massacre at Wounded Knee, most of the Lakota were rounded up and forced onto the Pine Ridge Agency. My grandfather and his wife had homesteaded

My great-grandfather, circa 1878

a remote area within the Badlands of South Dakota, on the reservation, but during World War I the U.S. Air Force reclaimed their homeland for bombing practice by the newly formed Ellsworth Air Force Base near Rapid City. Great-Grandfather was forced to relocate to the ranch that remains in my family today.

In my memory of that sunny summer morning, my grandfather got out of the truck and walked over to me holding a long cardboard box from Sears. He asked if my mom was around. I said "no," and he said he'd gotten me something. He handed me the box and I opened it to find a .410 shotgun, perfect for a scrawny kid like me. I'd already learned to shoot bottles off the hoods of cars with a .22 at the dump with my dad. Later that evening, we drove out along the tree line of the pasture, looking for pheasant and grouse. I bagged seven birds and helped clean them for dinner. Over time, I became a pretty good shot with rifles because I'd started so young, but those early days, after an outing, I remember cleaning out a lot of BB's from the pheasants we cooked.

My childhood summer days were long, dusty, and hot, and my cousins and I were perpetually covered in dirt from being outside as much as possible. Come midsummer, the timpsula was ready to harvest and we'd all pile into the back of my dad's truck. Windows down in the burning heat, we'd bounce across the pastures not following any roads. (The only car with air conditioning was my granddad's Caddy.) My dad was good at spotting the first plants, and as soon as he did, we'd start to see many more around us. In an old Lakota story, the timpsula, whose leaves look like little hands with five fingers, point to the next plant and we'd follow one to the next. We never dug up timpsula until after it had seeded and we always made sure to leave some in the ground. In

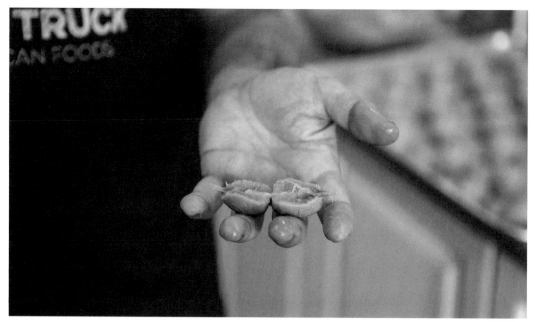

Timpsula

this way, we made sure the timpsula returned the following year. After the plant drops its seeds, it dries up and the top breaks off and blows away. So the window for harvesting is pretty short (as with all wild foods). We'd spend the afternoon in the baking sun, digging and tossing those roots into the back of the truck. It takes time and it's hard work, but all Lakota I know have a deep respect for timpsula and consider it worth the effort to collect, clean, and preserve this valuable food.

In this chapter, you'll find our favorite hearty dishes of fish, game, and vegetables. We share our methods for smoking and drying foods, adapting those ancient techniques to a modern kitchen. Although they're no longer needed to preserve foods, they help intensify flavors. These time-tried techniques are coming back into favor as we rediscover the wisdom of our forefathers.

WILD RICE

The first time I tasted wild rice, it was hand-harvested and came from the White Earth reservation in northern Minnesota. I was surprised by how different it is from cultivated black paddy rice. It cooks in 20 minutes and tastes slightly nutty, toasty, with hints of smoke and forest and the flintiness of those clear, cold lakes. Wild rice isn't "rice" at all, but the seed of an aquatic grass. In Ojibwe, it is *manoomin,* meaning "good berry" or "good seed," and the term may reflect a deeper meaning, suggesting "good, right, well."

Wild rice is extremely nutritious, with twice the amount of protein as brown rice, and it's far richer in vitamins than wheat, barley, oats, or rye. True wild rice swells to about four times its size as it cooks, earning the name "pocket money" among the early traders, who realized how just a handful could serve a lot of hungry men. Native Americans traditionally have served it many ways—cracked, popped, ground, and boiled into gruel for babies, simmered into hearty soups for the elderly, and brewed in life-giving teas for the sick. It is the one traditional food served at all important ceremonies, weddings, funerals, and births for the many tribes that have harvested it for centuries.

On Ojibwe reservations, the ricing season is called *manoominike-giizis* (Wild Ricing Moon). Today, the traditions continue with feasts of thanksgiving to honor the Great Spirit and the sacred nature of the rice. The idea of interrupting the natural reseeding and harvesting of rice is anathema to the Ojibwe. The harvest itself helps reseed the rice, as many of the grains miss the canoe and land in the water, and the Ojibwe believe that actually sowing the rice is offensive to Mother Earth. "Any attempt to sow the rice like whites sow corn would curse the lake, and the rice

Gathering wild rice, circa 1938

would never grow in it again," wrote Thomas Vennum in his book *Wild Rice and the Ojibway People.*

One early fall day, I went ricing with a friend on a lake so still and quiet that the only sound was that of my rice knockers tapping the seeds that rained into our canoe, of fish jumping, and the water lapping. Time stood still. I sensed how this ritual, these earthly rhythms, resounded through generations. Over the past few years, the search for wild, indigenous edibles has helped me see the natural world through an ancestor's eyes, to perceive more clearly the complex and beautiful web of food, history, and culture. The lifelong education is fulfilling beyond measure.

Freshly harvested rice is dried as soon as it comes off the lake. The traditional method is to spread the rice out to dry in the sun on woven mats, animal skins, or tarps. Birds help pick out the rice worms and spiders before the rice is parched or roasted in cast-iron pots set over a fire. Then, to remove the tight-fitting chaff from the rice kernel, the rice was traditionally "danced" on by young men wearing special moccasins. Once hulled, the wild rice was winnowed by tossing it about in a large birch-bark tray so that the wind could sweep the chaff off into the air. It was then ready to store.

Dancing on wild rice, with special moccasins

REAL WILD RICE
Psíŋ Ikčéka
Serves about 8

Because wild rice cooks so quickly and expands so fully, we always have cooked rice ready for a variety of salads, soups, stews, and cakes. Even after it's cooked, it will keep for several weeks in the refrigerator and freezes nicely.

This is our basic recipe. We'll often add a sprig of cedar to season the pot. As with our Wild Rice Cakes, page 63, we will intentionally overcook the cooked rice to make dough for pancakes, flatbreads, griddle cakes, and cookies. We also simmer the cooking water or "rice milk" down to concentrate its flavor for rice puddings and sorbet.

1 cup hand-harvested wild rice
4 cups water (or enough to cover the rice in the pot by 2 inches)
Salt to taste or wood ash

Wash the rice thoroughly by putting it into a colander and running it under cold water until the water runs clear. Turn the wild rice, water, and salt into a large, heavy saucepan and bring to a boil. Reduce the heat and simmer about 15 to 20 minutes.

Chef's Note: Season the cooking water with a small branch of cedar. Finish the rice with a sprinkling of juniper salt or maple syrup.

TATANKA TRUCK FRIED WILD RICE BOWL

Wakšíča Psíŋ Čheúŋpapi Ožúla

Serves 4 to 6

This popular Tatanka Truck item makes delicious use of cooked rice. We sizzle our "Dakota MirePoix" (a mix of minced squash, turnip, and wild onion or ramps), add the cooked rice, season with maple syrup, and serve with a variety of seasonal toppings.

2 tablespoons sunflower oil

½ cup minced squash (in winter use butternut; in summer use zucchini or summer squash)

½ cup minced turnip

1 cup chopped fresh wild onion or ramps

3 cups cooked wild rice

2 tablespoons maple syrup mixed with ⅓ cup water

Salt to taste

In a large skillet, heat the oil over medium high and sauté the squash, turnip, and onion until tender, about 5 to 8 minutes. Add the rice and cook for about 1 minute, then season with the maple syrup and salt. Serve topped with any or all of the following:

- Griddled Maple Squash, page 33
- Maple–Sage Roasted Vegetables, page 46
- Smoked Turkey, or other smoked meats, page 110
- Sunflower sprouts, page 174
- Wojape, page 173

Chef's Note: If using leeks instead of wild onion or ramps, substitute 1 leek, white part, cleaned and minced.

WILD RICE PILAF WITH WILD MUSHROOMS, ROASTED CHESTNUTS, AND DRIED CRANBERRIES

Psíŋ na Čhaŋnákpa na Úma Čheúŋpapi na Watȟókeča T'áǧa

Serves 4 to 6

Wild Rice Pilaf with Mushrooms, Roasted Chestnuts, and Dried Cranberries

Wild rice is a flavorful and remarkably satisfying food. The mushrooms add a dark, meaty flavor and texture, while the chestnuts are creamy (and high in protein). This meatless dish will appeal to omnivore and vegetarian alike. Cooked wild rice will keep several weeks in the refrigerator and for at least a year when frozen in a plastic freezer bag.

2 tablespoons sunflower or walnut oil

1 pound assorted mushrooms, cleaned

1 tablespoon chopped sage

½ cup chopped wild onion or shallots

½ cup Corn Stock, page 170, or vegetable stock

2 cups cooked wild rice

½ cup dried cranberries

1 cup roasted, peeled, chopped chestnuts*

1 tablespoon maple syrup to taste

½ to 1 teaspoon smoked salt to taste

In a large skillet, heat the oil over medium-high heat and add the mushrooms, sage, and onion. Cook, stirring, until the mushrooms are nicely browned and the onion is soft, about 5 minutes. Stir in the stock, wild rice, and cranberries and cook until the liquid is nearly evaporated. Stir in the roasted chestnuts. Season with maple syrup and smoked salt to taste.

*To roast and peel chestnuts, use the sharp point of a small knife to score an X on the flat side of the chestnut and place on a baking sheet. Roast in a 350°F oven until the skins begin to peel back. The length of roasting time will depend on the freshness and size of the chestnuts and range from about 10 to 25 minutes. Remove, and when cool enough to handle, peel.

MUSHROOMS

The summer I worked for the Forest Service, I learned about mushrooms from one of our crew members who could identify all of them. We'd bring her samples each day and she'd sort through the edibles. Later, in Minneapolis, foragers would arrive at our restaurant's back door with boxes of morels, chanterelles, trumpets, and cèpes. All across the north woods (and especially on Madeline Island, in Lake Superior), chicken of the woods and black trumpets pop up throughout the spring, summer, and fall, after rain.

Chanterelles

TIMPSULA CAKES
WITH CEDAR-BRAISED BEANS

Thíŋpsila Aǧúyapi Sáka na Omníča Lolóbyapi
Serves 4 to 6

There is nothing truly close to the flavor of fresh timpsula, but because it's a wild root, specific to the prairies and difficult to obtain, we've created this version of cakes using turnips and butternut squash, mashed and then griddled. Top these with Cedar-Braised Beans, page 36, and Griddled Maple Squash, page 33, for a satisfying vegetarian dish.

TIMPSULA

Timpsula's roots are covered with a thick brown bark that, once peeled, reveals a pale white vegetable about the size of a chicken egg. Timpsula has a distinct taste, sweet and crisp when very fresh with a flavor often described as unroasted peanuts. When I was a kid, we ate it raw or cut into chunks roasted or simmered. We'd braid the tops of the plants to hang and dry in the sun. Once they are dried, we boil them into a porridge or add chips of timpsula to soups and grind it into flour to use as a thickener or bake into bread.

6 timpsula, cut into chunks (or 4 medium turnips plus 1 small butternut squash, peeled, seeded, all cut into chunks)

Water to cover

1 small sprig cedar

Pinch salt to taste

Pinch crushed juniper to taste

2 to 3 tablespoons hazelnut or sunflower oil or Rendered Duck Fat, page 105, plus extra for greasing the pan

1 cup Cedar-Braised Beans, page 36

1 cup Griddled Maple Squash, page 33

½ cup toasted sunflower seeds, page 158

Put the timpsula (or turnip and squash) and cedar in a large pot and add water to just cover. Set over high heat, bring to a boil, reduce to a simmer, and cook until the vegetables are very tender, about 15 to 20 minutes. Drain off any excess water and place in a bowl. Mash with the oil and season with the salt and juniper. When the mash has cooled a little, form patties about 4 inches in diameter and 2 inches thick.

Film a large skillet with the remaining oil and set over medium-high heat. Sear the patties until lightly browned and crisped on both sides, about 5 minutes per side. Serve topped with Cedar-Braised Beans, Griddled Maple Squash, and sunflower seeds.

SMOKED WHITEFISH OR TROUT

Hoğáŋ Ašótkaziyapi
Serves 4 to 6 (or more as an appetizer)

In the old days, smoking fish fresh was a group effort. In Minnesota, for instance, there would be many helping to catch fish, and more people on the shore helping to process the catch immediately. The fish heads and spines would be removed, leaving the tail intact, holding together the two fillets. The fish heads and spines would be immediately used to make soup to feed the workers, and the fillets would then be flipped inside out, so the skin is on the inside, and the meat would be scored a few times. Then the fish would be hung on sticks and placed over a low-heat fire with lots of smoke and occasionally turned to evenly preserve. Preserving the fish immediately was key to flavor and you can still see this preservation method being used along the West Coast of the United States all the way up to Alaska and in North Atlantic countries such as Iceland, Greenland, and Northern Europe.

We are using a more modern technique with brining as the first step. Be sure the fish is thoroughly cleaned before you begin.

½ cup coarse salt
2 tablespoons maple syrup
1 quart water
2 pounds trout, whitefish, or walleye fillets, 3 to 5 ounces each, pin bones removed and skin on

In a 4-quart container, stir together the salt, maple syrup, and water until the salt is thoroughly dissolved. Add the fillets; they should be submerged. Cover and refrigerate for about 3 hours.

Remove the fillets from the brine, rinse thoroughly, pat dry, place, skin side down, on a cooling rack (set over a sheet pan to catch any drips). Continue to dry the fish in the refrigerator for at least 24 hours, or until the skin is tacky to the touch.

Bring a smoker to 160°F. Put the fish onto the smoking racks, skin side down, about ½ inch apart. Smoke until the fish is cooked through and has darkened in color, about 2½ to 3 hours. The fish can be stored in an airtight container for up to a week.

Chef's Note: Save the skins of the smoked fish. They are delicious when griddled and cut into strips for garnishing a soup. They can also be topped with smoked fish, griddled vegetables, greens, and berries.

Smoked fish

WILD RICE–CRUSTED WALLEYE

Hoğáŋ

Serves 4 to 6

Wild Rice-Crusted Walleye

The Red Lake Nation is an Ojibwe community in northern Minnesota, home of our ethnobotanist Tashia, who shares her knowledge with our team. In the late fall of 2015 we participated in an Indigenous Sustainable Food Summit focused on our region's Native heirloom varieties of corn, beans, and squash, and Red Lake's wild rice, smoked fish, and game. We source all of our fish—the walleye, northerns, and whitefish—from the Red Lake Nation Fishery. The Red Lake community protects its beautiful and pristine waters by fishing sustainably.

For an impressive presentation, butterfly the fish (so that it's filleted but whole and served head on). Garnish with fresh cranberries, chopped apple, or berries lightly tossed into the pan, right before serving. This recipe works nicely with trout, too.

4 to 6 walleye or trout fillets, or butterflied fish
½ cup Wild Rice Flour, page 167, or finely ground cornmeal
Pinch smoked salt
Pinch crushed juniper berries
¼ cup sunflower oil, or more as needed

Rinse the fillets, remove any pin bones, and pat dry. Pour the wild rice flour onto a flat plate and stir in the smoked salt and juniper. Dredge both sides of the fillets in the seasoned flour to thoroughly coat.

Heat the oil in a large skillet over a high flame. Without crowding the pan, fry one or two of the fillets in the oil for about 2 to 4 minutes per side until nicely crisped and cooked through. Drain on paper towels and serve immediately.

RED LAKE WALLEYE— THE GOOD FISH STORY

Walleye is a firm, delicate, flaky white fish that tastes of the flinty cold waters of northern Minnesota. The state's largest commercial fishery is on the shores of Red Lake, run by the Nation that bears its name. The Red Lake Band of Chippewa is a "closed reservation" where all land is held in common by the tribe. Ojibwe is the official language. The Red Lake Nation Fishery owes its success to cooperation between the state, the Department of Natural Resources, and the tribe.

By the 1990s, overfishing had devastated the lake's walleye population, so all parties involved agreed in 1997 to a ten-year moratorium on fishing. Over the next six years, massive stocking efforts added about forty million fry to the lake. Today, netting is banned and the Fishery mission is to sustainably manage, harvest, and prepare the lake's fish for sale—walleye, yellow perch, crappie, northern, plus smoked whitefish. It will ship fresh and frozen fish to just about any place in the country.

HERB-ROASTED FISH

Hoğáŋ Čheúŋpapi
Serves 4 to 6

Chef Brian Yazzie, our chef de cuisine, is a citizen of the Navajo Nation who shares his traditions and his family's recipes with the team. The original recipe for this dish calls for the bluehead sucker fish, a rare fish specific to the Southwest, but any small or large firm fish works nicely.

The fish is traditionally cooked in a pit filled with hot wood coals, covered with sand so that it steam-roasts. Although not nearly as dramatic, nearly similar results can be achieved using a clay pot. Be sure to soak the pot for a good hour before cooking. Set the oven to a low temperature.

1 large whitefish, about 4 to 5 pounds
Coarse salt
Sumac
3 to 4 sprigs sage
4 to 5 wild onions or shallots cut into quarters
3 dozen corn husks, soaked, for the traditional pit method

Generously sprinkle the outside and the cavities of the fish with the salt and sumac. Stuff the cavities of the fish with the sage and the onions. If using the traditional pit method, wrap the fish in enough of the soaked corn husks to completely cover the fish.

To cook the fish in a traditional pit: Cover the bottom of a 1-foot-deep pit (2 feet in diameter) with hot wood coals. Set the corn husk–wrapped fish on the coals. Fill the pit with sand to cover the fish. Steam/cook the fish for 45 minutes to 1 hour. Dig away the sand. Remove the fish from the pit. Set on a platter. Serve the fish whole, family style.

To cook the fish in a clay pot: Soak the pot in water for a good hour. Place the fish in the clay pot. Cover and place in a 250°F oven and cook the fish for about 1 hour or until it is tender. Remove the clay pot from the oven. Remove the fish and serve family style.

TATANKA TRUCK
SUNFLOWER-CRUSTED TROUT
Serves 4 to 6

This crispy trout with a sunflower crust is one of chef Vern DeFoe's recipes and a Tatanka Truck favorite. Vern, a member of the Red Cliff Band of Lake Superior Chippewa, serves the trout with roe on wild rice flatbread, garnished with dried apple slices.

4 to 6 trout fillets
½ cup ground untoasted sunflower seeds
1 to 2 tablespoons ground sumac
Pinch smoked salt
2 to 3 tablespoons sunflower oil

Rinse the fillets, remove any pin bones, and pat dry. On a flat plate, mix together the sunflower seeds, sumac, and smoked salt. Dredge both sides of the fillets in the seasoned mixture to thoroughly coat.

Heat the oil in a large skillet over a high flame. Without crowding the pan, fry one or two of the fillets in the oil for about 2 to 4 minutes per side, until nicely crisped and cooked through. Drain on paper towels and serve immediately.

CATTAILS

Foraging for cattails

Cattail has been an important staple of foraged foods. It is found all over the world, and every part of the plant is edible at different times of the year. It's easy to identify and easy to harvest (as long as you don't mind getting your feet muddy). Nicknamed "Defender of the Shoreline," cattails protect the shore from wave erosion and help filter the water from contaminants, all while providing greens, buds, spikes, and roots that make good eating. In early spring, just after the cattails have begun to grow, they have a green bloom-spike covered with a thin husk. Once peeled, the bulbs are delicious sautéed or boiled and seasoned. Once the shoots grow up, they can be peeled and cooked like asparagus. Later, the flower may be boiled (when still young) and eaten like a mini corn on the cob. Cattail pollen makes a very pretty golden seasoning. The cattail roots or rhizomes are starchy and can be dried and ground into flour and used to make biscuits; but that's a lot of work, and, to be honest, I prefer the upper parts of the plant.

Cattail corns

GROUSE WITH CRANBERRY AND SAGE

Čháŋšiyo nakúŋ Gmá na Pheží ȟota Iyúlthǔŋ

Serves 4

Grouse, such as partridge, feed on wild berries, nuts, and seeds. Near the cranberry regions of southern Wisconsin, the wild berries turn the bird's meat bright pink. In this recipe, the rendered duck fat, cranberries, and sage baste the meat while it roasts to become tender and flavorful. This is great on our Wild Rice Pilaf, page 84.

2 dressed grouse, about 1 pound each

Coarse salt

1 tart apple

8 sprigs sage

¼ cup cranberries

2 tablespoons maple syrup

¼ cup walnuts, toasted

½ cup Rendered Duck Fat, page 105, or sunflower oil

1 tablespoon chopped sage

1 wild onion or shallot, minced

Water or cider as needed

Preheat the oven to 350°F. Rinse the birds and pat dry with paper towels. Sprinkle them inside and out with the salt. Core the apple and cut into quarters. Place 2 quarters of apple and 4 sprigs of sage into each bird's cavity.

In a small saucepan, cook the cranberries with the maple syrup over low heat until the cranberries pop, about 3 minutes. Put the berries, walnuts, duck fat, sage, and onion into a food processor fitted with a steel blade and process until combined. Tuck some of the mixture under the breast skin of the birds and rub the remaining mixture over the birds. Set breast side up on a roasting rack set over a roasting pan. Add about 2 inches of cider or water into the pan. Roast the grouse, basting frequently with the pan juices, until the birds are nicely browned, the juices run clear, and a meat thermometer inserted into the thigh registers 155°F. Remove and allow to stand at least 10 minutes. Carve and serve with the pan juices drizzled over all.

Maple–Juniper Roast Pheasant, griddled apple

MAPLE–JUNIPER ROAST PHEASANT

Čhaŋháŋpi Tiktíča na Ȟaŋté úŋ Šiyóša Čheúŋpapi

Serves 4 to 6

When I was growing up on the Pine Ridge Reservation, we stocked our freezers with pheasant and grouse. We'd see them darting across the dirt roads into the dry brush. They were as common as the red-winged blackbirds perched on the fence posts.

Overnight dry brining seasons and helps this especially lean bird to become tender and succulent. The technique also works with grouse and guinea hens.

2 small pheasants

1 tablespoon coarse salt

2 tablespoons maple sugar

1 teaspoon sumac

1 teaspoon crushed juniper

¼ cup Rendered Duck Fat, page 105, or sunflower oil

1 cup fresh cranberries

½ cup Corn or Turkey Stock, pages 170, or vegetable stock

3 tablespoons maple vinegar

2 griddled apple halves for garnish (optional)

The day before, rinse the pheasants and pat dry with paper towels. To dry-brine, generously season with the salt, maple sugar, sumac, and juniper. Place on a roasting pan or deep plate in the refrigerator, uncovered, overnight.

Preheat the oven to 500°F. Place the pheasants breast side up in a medium roasting pan. Rub a generous amount of the duck fat under the skin of the birds and over the outside of the skin. Put half the cranberries into the cavity of the pheasants and spread the rest in the pan. Pour the stock and vinegar into the roasting pan. Roast for 15 minutes. Reduce the heat to 350°F and baste the pheasants with the pan juices. Continue roasting until the skin is crisp, the juices run clear, and a meat thermometer inserted in the thigh reaches 155°F, about 30 to 45 more minutes. Allow to stand at least 10 minutes before carving.

Carve and drizzle with the pan juices before serving with the griddled apples.

- Substitute 2 tablespoons cider vinegar and 1 tablespoon maple syrup for the maple vinegar.
- For the griddled apples, slice the apples in half horizontally, brush with a little sunflower or walnut oil, and griddle cut side down in a hot skillet or frying pan until lightly browned, about 3 to 5 minutes.

SWEET AND SOUR ROAST GOOSE WITH AUTUMN SQUASH AND CRANBERRIES

Čhaŋháŋpi Tiktíča úŋ Maǧá Čheúŋpapi nakúŋ Wagmú na Watȟókeča T'áǧa
Serves 6 to 8

This slow-roasted goose will emerge from the oven golden brown and tender. The sauce was inspired by an older recipe using "sour sap," a vinegar made from the maple syrup's last run blended with the maple syrup. Save the fat that collects at the bottom of the roasting pan for cooking vegetables, frying corn cakes, or sautéing other meats.

This recipe works equally well with duck if you adjust the cooking time accordingly.

1 whole goose, about 10 pounds
Coarse salt
Pinch crushed juniper
1 large butternut squash (about 4 pounds, peeled, seeded, and cut into 2-inch chunks)
1 cup cranberries
¼ cup maple syrup
2 tablespoons maple vinegar
1 teaspoon coarse mustard

Rinse and dry the goose with paper towels. Rub it inside and out with the salt and refrigerate, uncovered, for at least 6 hours or overnight. Then pat it dry with paper towels, set it on a rack, and allow it to come to room temperature, about an hour. Trim any excess fat from the goose and reserve for another use. Using the tip of a sharp knife, lightly score the breast and leg skin in a crosshatch pattern. This helps to render the fat more quickly during roasting.

Preheat the oven to 325°F. Season the goose with a little more salt and the ground juniper. Place the goose on a rack in a deep roasting pan and roast for about an hour. Every 30 minutes or so, baste the bird with the pan juices; then pour off the fat through a sieve into a large heatproof bowl (and reserve it for later use). Reduce the heat to 275°F, add the cubed squash and cranberries to the pan, and return the goose to the oven. Continue roasting until a thermometer registers 165°F at the center of the breast, about 1½ to 2 hours. Total roasting time is about 3 hours.

In a small dish, whisk together the maple syrup, vinegar, and mustard to make a glaze. Brush the goose with the glaze several minutes before removing it from the oven. When it is done, place the goose on a carving board and allow to rest for 20 to 30 minutes before carving. Serve the goose with the squash and cranberries drizzled with the pan juices.

SAGE AND ROSE-HIP ROASTED DUCK
Phežíȟota na Uŋžíŋžiŋtka úŋ Maǧáksiča Čheúŋpapi
Serves 4 to 6

The ducks we bagged when I was growing up were wild ducks; some were puddle ducks, others were diving ducks that varied in size. Their flavor depends on where the duck had been feeding. Shallow-water ducks that feed on local grains tend to be succulent, while diving ducks that eat fish can taste, well, fishy. We've found that an overnight soak in brine benefits any duck, wild or domestic. This simple recipe yields a duck with supercrisp skin and juicy meat. The sage and rose-hip sauce is tangy, woodsy, and mildly sweet. Serve over wild rice.

1 5- to 6-pound duck
1 tablespoon coarse salt
1 tablespoon crushed juniper
1 large sprig sage
½ cup dried rose hips
Water to cover
1 tablespoon chopped sage
2 tablespoons honey

Preheat the oven to 425°F. Cut off the wing tips of the duck with poultry shears or a sharp knife. Remove any excess fat from the neck and body cavity. Rinse inside and out and pat dry with a paper towel or a clean dishcloth. Prick the outer layer of fat with a sharp fork or knife. Sprinkle the salt and juniper over the duck, outside and inside the cavity. Put the sprig of sage inside the cavity of the duck.

Place the duck in a roasting pan and roast, breast side up, for 45 minutes, then remove from the oven and flip it over so that the back is up. Return to the oven and continue roasting another 45 minutes. Remove and turn it over so the breast side is up once more. Continue roasting until the duck is fully cooked and an instant-read thermometer inserted into the thigh registers 165°F, another 35 to 50 minutes. Allow the duck to rest before carving.

To make the sauce: Put the rose hips into a small saucepan and add just enough water to cover. Set over medium heat, bring to a simmer, and cook until the rose hips are plump and soft. Strain off and discard the rose hips, retaining the cooking liquid, and return to the stove. Add the chopped sage and season with the honey, to taste. Drizzle the sage and rose-hip sauce over the cooked duck and serve.

SEARED DUCK BREAST WITH CIDER GLAZE

Maǧáksiča Tȟaspáŋhaŋpi Akáštaŋpi

Serves 4 to 6

Seared Duck Breast with Cider Glaze, Wild Rice Cake, Amaranth Cracker

In this recipe, the duck breast is barely cooked, seared under a maple glaze, and served over a griddled corn cake with wild mushrooms and a wild pesto. It's a simple plate that makes a stunning entrée. Unless you hunt or know someone who does, find duck breasts in the freezer section of most grocery stores. The sear on high heats gets the skin nice and crispy. Serve on Corn Cakes, page 51, or Wild Rice Pilaf, page 84.

1 teaspoon coarse mineral salt

Pinch sumac

Pinch crushed juniper

2 to 3 pounds duck breasts, skin on

1 to 2 tablespoons sunflower or hazelnut oil

1 cup cider

1 tablespoon chopped sage

1 tablespoon maple vinegar

1 tablespoon maple syrup, or to taste

Wojape for garnish

In a large, self-sealing plastic bag, shake the salt, sumac, and juniper together, then add the duck breasts and shake to coat with the mix. Seal and refrigerate at least 1 hour or overnight. Remove from the refrigerator and bring to room temperature.

Preheat the oven to 400°F. In a large ovenproof sauté pan, add enough oil to generously cover the pan and set over medium-high heat until shimmering. Working in batches so not to crowd the pan, sear the duck breasts, skin side down, for about 5 minutes. Turn and sear the other side for 5 minutes. Place the pan in the oven and roast for about 5 to 7 minutes for medium rare. Transfer the breasts to a plate and tent to keep warm.

Pour all but about 1 teaspoon of fat from the pan and reserve for another use. Return the pan to medium heat, add the cider, and scrape up the browned bits from the bottom of the pan. Stir in the sage. Simmer the cider to reduce by half. Add the vinegar and cook to reduce for several more minutes. Season with the maple syrup. Cut the duck breasts into 1-inch-thick diagonal slices and serve drizzled with the Wojape sauce.

RENDERING DUCK OR GOOSE FAT

Rendering the fat from duck or goose is easy and the rendered fat is the best cooking medium for just about any fried food. It's incredibly tasty with a silky mouth-feel and yields a bonus—little fritters or cracklings. Be warned, though, the freshly crisped morsels are addictive! They're terrific sprinkled on salads, over corn cakes, and on top of wild rice.

To render fat from a duck or goose: Carefully remove all the skin and fat from the duck, cutting close to but not touching the meat. Cut the skin and fat into inch-size chunks and place in a heavy-bottomed stockpot or Dutch oven. Add ¾ cup water. Set over medium-low heat and bring to a simmer, turning the bits of skin occasionally, until the water has evaporated and the skin has fully crisped and released the fat, about 1 hour. Remove the cracklings with a slotted spoon and drain on paper towels. Store in an airtight container at room temperature for up to 3 days or freeze.

Allow the fat to cool slightly, then strain through a fine-mesh sieve lined with cheesecloth into clean containers with lids. The fat may be stored, covered, up to 6 months in the refrigerator or frozen.

CRISPY DUCK LEGS

Maǧáksiča Hú Gaǧáyapi
Serves 4 to 6

This recipe is an easier, quicker, and less fussy method of making "confit." The legs are cured for 24 hours and then cooked for about 4 hours in their own rendered fat. Serve these on a bed of Real Wild Rice, page 81, Maple–Sage Roasted Vegetables, page 46, or Three Sisters Mash, page 43.

1 to 2 teaspoons coarse salt
½ teaspoon crushed juniper
½ teaspoon ground sage
Pinch sumac
4 to 8 duck legs, depending on size, rinsed and patted dry but not trimmed

In a small bowl, combine the salt, juniper, sage, and sumac and sprinkle the duck legs generously with the mix. Place the duck legs in a pan, cover tightly with plastic, and refrigerate for 24 hours.

Preheat the oven to 325°F. Place the duck legs fat side down in a large oven-proof skillet, with the legs fitting snugly together, or use two skillets.

Set the skillet over medium-high heat and cook until the fat begins to render, about 20 minutes. Turn the legs over, cover the pan with foil, and place in the oven.

Roast for 2 hours, remove the foil, and continue roasting until the duck is golden, 1 more hour. Remove the duck and reserve the fat.

Serve the duck legs warm over cooked wild rice, roasted vegetables, or Three Sisters Mash, page 43.

DUCK PÂTÉ, WITH DRIED APPLE

Magaksica Yulopapi nakun Thapanhapnpi Thaspan Pusyapi

Serves 4 to 6

Delicious served by itself, and on Corn Cakes, page 51, or with Amaranth Crackers, page 60.

3 tablespoons rendered duck fat, page 105

1 wild onion or shallot, chopped

1 duck liver, cut into 1-inch pieces

½ teaspoon chopped sage

Generous pinch salt

Pinch crushed juniper

¼ cup cider

4 to 6 slices fresh or Dried Apple, page 177, for garnish

Place the duck fat in a skillet and set over medium-high heat to melt, about 4 to 5 minutes. Add the onion or shallot and cook for 30 seconds, stirring occasionally. Add the liver, sage, salt, and juniper. Cook, stirring occasionally, until the liver is cooked through and no longer pink, about 5 minutes. Add the cider and continue cooking to reduce to a glaze, about 3 minutes.

Transfer to a food processor fitted with a steel blade and process into a rough pâté. Place in a bowl and allow to cool. Store, covered in the refrigerator, until ready to use. Serve garnished with the apple slices.

DUCK AND WILD RICE PEMMICAN

Maǧáksiča na Psíŋ Wasná
Serves 4 to 6

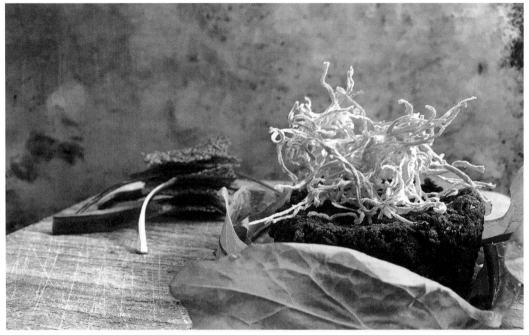

Duck and Wild Rice Pemmican

Pemmican, like the wasna I grew up with, is an ancient staple of dried meat, tallow, berries, and other seasonings. Our take on this dish using flavor-intense duck speaks of culture and history in a bite. This duck appetizer is rich, satisfying, and surprisingly easy. Although it takes a little time and patience for the duck to dry in either a dehydrator or in a very low temperature oven, the recipe comes together in a snap. Serve as finger food, on a bed of greens, or even with dried vegetable chips for a starter or light meal.

2 duck breasts, skin on
4 tablespoons maple sugar
1 tablespoon salt
⅓ cup uncooked wild rice, page 79
½ cup dried blueberries

Carefully remove all the skin and fat from the duck breasts, cutting close to, but not touching, the meat. Once the fat and skin are removed, cut into 1-inch chunks. Place the skin, with its fat, into a heavy-bottomed skillet or Dutch oven. Set the pan over low heat and slowly cook, stirring occasionally, until the skin has crisped and its fat has changed to liquid, about 45 minutes. With a slotted spoon, remove the crisped skin (cracklings) and drain them in a bowl lined with paper towels. Allow the liquid fat to cool to room temperature, then strain through a fine-mesh sieve lined with cheesecloth into a bowl or a clean glass jar.

In a small bowl, mix together the sugar and salt.

Slice the duck breast into thin, long strips along the grain. Rub both sides of the duck strips with the sugar and salt. If you have a food dehydrator, follow the instructions for making jerky.

To dry the duck in the oven: Preheat the oven to the lowest setting. Lay the strips on a wire rack over a rimmed baking sheet and put into the oven. Leave the meat until it is dried out but still pliable, about 6 to 8 hours.

In a medium skillet, heat 1 tablespoon of the rendered duck fat, or more as needed, over low and add the wild rice. Shake the pan until the rice begins to "pop" and "puff." Spread the rice out on a paper towel. Reserve 1 tablespoon of the puffed rice for garnish.

Put the cracklings, dried duck, puffed wild rice (except for the reserved amount), dried blueberries, and any leftover duck oil into a food processor fitted with a steel blade. Pulse to chop fine. Put the mixture in a bowl and, using 2 tablespoons or ⅛ cup, form the mixture into small bites. Serve garnished with the puffed wild rice.

SMOKED DUCK OR PHEASANT
Maǧáksiča naíŋš Šiyóša Ašótkaziyapi
Serves 4 to 6

Pheasant and duck are wonderful smoked. Brining helps make them more juicy and tender, and the smoking process adds the flavor of an open flame. Brining does two things: it seasons meat and, through osmosis, helps infuse moisture to keep it juicy. We leave the skin on the birds to help keep them from drying out. (Many markets now sell pheasant, often frozen.)

Shred the smoked pheasant or duck and serve over Corn Cakes, page 51, or Timpsula Cakes, page 86, with a drizzle of Wojape. Plan on a 12-hour brine followed by a 5-hour smoke.

2 3-pound pheasants or 1 5- to 6-pound duck
¼ cup salt
¼ cup maple sugar
4 cups water
2 cups maple syrup, boiled down to 1 cup

Rinse and thoroughly clean the pheasants or duck. In a large container, stir together the salt, sugar, and water until dissolved. Immerse the birds in the container and brine in the refrigerator for at least 12 and up to 18 hours. Remove and pat dry; allow them to sit for 1 to 3 hours, until the skin is dry to the touch.

Smoke the birds over hard wood (hickory) for at least 3 hours at 200° to 250°F. After 1 hour, baste with the maple syrup every 30 minutes. The cooking time will vary greatly depending on the size and type of bird. Use an instant-read thermometer to check for doneness. It should read 160°F when the birds are ready. Remove to a cooling rack, baste one more time, and cool.

Chef's Note: The smoked duck or pheasant makes a fine stuffing for Tamales, page 57, and in any soups.

ROAST TURKEY, WILD ONIONS, MAPLE SQUASH, AND CRANBERRY SAUCE

Waglékšuŋ, Pšíŋ, Wagmú, nakúŋ Watȟókeča T'áǧa Yužápi

Serves 8

Hands down, this is the best way to roast turkey. We serve it and the vegetables over wild rice. Save the turkey bones for stock, page 170.

1 small (10- to 12-pound) turkey, rinsed well and patted dry
¼ cup hazelnut oil
2 tablespoons chopped sage
Coarse salt
Crushed juniper
2 cups Corn, Wild Rice, or Turkey Stock, page 170
4 wild onions or 2 large onions, quartered
1 cup wild mushrooms, chopped
2 cups cubed winter squash
⅛ cup maple syrup
Cranberry Sauce, page 108

One hour before roasting, remove the turkey from the refrigerator and bring to room temperature. In a blender, puree the hazelnut oil and sage and rub over the turkey. Season with salt and juniper.

Preheat the oven to 450°F. Place the turkey into a roasting pan, add the stock, and put into the oven. Roast until the turkey is light golden brown, about 45 minutes. Reduce the oven temperature to 350°F and continue roasting. After about 1½ hours, scatter the onions, mushrooms, and squash into the roasting pan and baste the turkey and the vegetables occasionally with the pan juices. Continue cooking until an instant-read thermometer inserted into the thigh registers 160°F, about 30 minutes to 1 hour longer. Brush the turkey with the maple syrup.

Remove the turkey from the oven and transfer to a cutting board. Arrange the vegetables on a platter. Carve the turkey and arrange over the vegetables. Drizzle the pan juices over all. Serve with wild rice and Cranberry Sauce.

CRANBERRY SAUCE

Watȟókeča T'áǧa Yužápi
Makes 1½ cups

Use this to drizzle over roasted squash or turkey, on Wild Rice Cakes, page 63, or for a dessert sauce.

1½ cups cranberries, fresh or frozen
¼ cup cider
¼ cup maple syrup
Salt to taste
Crushed juniper to taste

Put all the ingredients into a saucepan and set over medium heat. Bring to a simmer, stirring occasionally, and cook until the cranberries have popped and the mixture is thick. Remove from the heat and put into a fine-mesh sieve set over a bowl. Press the mixture firmly with the back of a spoon and scrape the underside of the sieve to capture all of the fruit pulp. Taste and adjust the seasoning. Serve warm or cool.

CIDER-BRAISED TURKEY THIGHS

Tȟaspáŋhaŋpi na Phežíȟota úŋ Waglékšuŋ Lolóbyapi

Serves 4 to 6

With dark, rich meat and a coarse texture, turkey thighs are reminiscent of game birds. This recipe makes a nice weeknight dinner served with smashed sweet potatoes or maple squash, corn cakes, or wild rice.

3 tablespoons sunflower oil
2 to 3 pounds turkey thighs, skin removed
1 cup chopped wild onion
1 cup Corn, Wild Rice, or Game Stock, page 170
½ cup cider
¼ cup maple or apple cider vinegar
2 whole juniper berries
4 sage leaves
1 large apple, cored, seeded, and diced

Heat the oil over medium-high heat in a Dutch oven or heavy pot. Brown the thighs on all sides, about 3 minutes per side. Remove the thighs and set aside. Reduce the heat and add the onion and cook until softened, about 3 to 5 minutes.

Add the stock and cider, increase the heat, and bring to a boil, scraping any browned bits from the bottom of the pan. Stir in the remaining ingredients and return the thighs to the pot. Reduce the heat to a simmer. Cover the pot and cook the turkey, turning occasionally, adding more stock if the liquid becomes low, until the turkey is very tender, about 45 minutes. Remove the turkey from the pot and set aside, covered to keep it warm. Skim the fat from the surface of the liquid in the pot, raise the heat to bring to a boil, and reduce the liquid by half. Taste and adjust the seasoning. Serve the thighs with the sauce drizzled on top.

MAPLE-BRINED SMOKED TURKEY
Waglékšuŋ Ašótkaziyapi
Serves 10 to 12

The traditional American Thanksgiving meal showcases the bounty of indigenous foods and the influence Native Americans have had on U.S. cuisine. But this national holiday is fraught with the tragic history of colonialism. To me, the myth of Natives and colonists happily sharing a feast ignores the true story of the atrocities, genocide, and forced migration our people suffered at the hands of Europeans. This is why so few Native Americans celebrate the holiday. Many do gather, however, in a ritual giving of thanks for the harvest and to honor their ancestors. Our family and friends cook a meal of squash, wild rice, and turkey all seasoned with indigenous flavors. This recipe ensures a terrific, tender, juicy turkey for dinner, and leftover turkey meat is delicious on Corn Cakes, page 51, and added to the Smoked Turkey and Acorn Soup, page 71.

10-pound turkey with giblets removed
4 quarts water
1 cup coarse salt
½ cup maple syrup
2 tablespoons whole juniper berries
1 large sprig sage
4 to 6 cups wood chips (hickory, apple, or hazelnut)
Sunflower oil for rubbing the turkey

Place the turkey in a large container (a food-safe bucket or big pot). In a saucepan, heat about 1 quart of the water with the salt until it dissolves. Cool. Then add the salt water, the remaining water, maple syrup, juniper berries, and sage to the turkey. Make sure the turkey is fully submerged. Cover (weigh the turkey down, if necessary) and refrigerate for 12 to 24 hours. Soak the wood chips in cold water for at least 4 hours or overnight. Remove the turkey and pat dry.

Prepare a charcoal grill or smoker for indirect heat, at about 275°F. Sprinkle in enough of the soaked wood chips to cover the coals and allow them to char.

Place the turkey in a roasting pan fitted with a rack. Brush the turkey with the sunflower oil. Place the turkey in the grill or smoker and cook until the internal temperature of the thigh registers 165°F, about 3½ to 4½ hours. Remove and allow to rest for at least 20 minutes before carving.

RABBIT

It's common lore that rabbit tastes like chicken. But rabbit meat is more delicate, a little drier, denser, and slightly sweeter than chicken. It's delicious and easy to cook.

Rabbits are easy to raise and abundant in the wild (and backyards), so why don't we see more rabbit meat in supermarkets? Maybe because rabbits are not easy to process on a commercial scale, and they're bony and very lean. Perhaps as the local food movement continues to prosper and demand rises, we'll see more rabbit dishes in family-style restaurants and home kitchens.

Saddle of Rabbit with Hazelnuts and Raspberry–Rose Hip Sauce, Wasna, hazelnuts

The best method for cooking rabbit is a slow braise or simple stew. To add richness and color to the dish, it's best to brown the meat prior to simmering in liquid for a long time.

To joint a rabbit: Detach the legs from the carcass by cutting through the muscle on the front of the leg; otherwise the leg will toughen as it cooks. Cut around the forelegs and remove them. Cut the saddle into several pieces to serve.

Rabbit

OLD-FASHIONED RABBIT STEW

Eháŋni Iyéčhel Maštíŋča Waháŋpi
Serve 4 to 6

Serve this over golden Corn Mush, page 59, for a comforting winter meal. The long, slow cooking time is especially good for a wild rabbit. If rabbit is not available, substitute turkey thighs.

3 tablespoons corn flour
2 teaspoons dried oregano or bergamot
Pinch sumac
Pinch smoked salt
1 large rabbit, about 3 pounds, cut into 8 pieces
3 tablespoons sunflower oil
3 wild onions or 2 large onions, coarsely chopped
3 cups Corn, Rabbit, or Turkey Stock, page 170
1 cup soaked hominy

Put the flour, oregano, and a generous pinch of sumac and smoked salt in a large freezer bag. Add the rabbit portions to the bag, a few at a time, and shake well until evenly coated in the seasoned flour. Transfer to a plate.

Heat the oil in a large, heavy pot set over medium heat. Fry the rabbit a few pieces at a time, until golden brown all over. Put the pieces into a baking dish. Add the onions to the pot and sauté until lightly browned and beginning to soften, about 5 minutes. Pour 1 cup of the stock into the cooking pot and stir vigorously to deglaze any of the browned bits at the bottom of the pot. Simmer for a few seconds then add the remaining stock and the hominy. Return the rabbit to the pot, partially cover, and set over medium heat. Bring to a boil, reduce the heat, and simmer, turning the rabbit pieces occasionally, until the meat is very tender, about 2 to 2½ hours. Skim off and discard any fat that rises to the top as the rabbit cooks. Serve the rabbit stew over corn mush or wild rice.

Rabbit Braised with Apples and Mint

RABBIT BRAISED WITH APPLES AND MINT

Tȟaspáŋ na Čheyáka nakúŋ Maštíŋča Lolóbyapi
Serves 4 to 6

This simple skillet meal is delicious served over wild rice, corn cakes, or cooked hominy. If rabbit is not available, substitute turkey or chicken thighs.

1 large rabbit, about 3 pounds, cut into pieces
Coarse salt
2 tablespoons sunflower or vegetable oil
2 wild onions, ramps, or large shallots
3 sage leaves, chopped
4 mint leaves, chopped
½ cup cider
½ cup Corn or Rabbit Stock, page 170
2 tablespoons maple syrup
1 tablespoon maple vinegar
1 large apple, cored and sliced

Season the rabbit with the salt. Heat the oil in a large skillet over medium heat. Cook the rabbit until browned on all sides, about 6 minutes per side. Transfer the rabbit to a plate. Add the onions, sage, and mint and cook until tender, about 3 to 5 minutes. Add the cider and stock and scrape up any dark bits sticking to the bottom of the pan. Drizzle in the maple syrup and vinegar. Cover the pan and braise until tender, about 45 minutes to 1 hour, turning the pieces occasionally. Uncover, add the apples, and continue cooking, basting the rabbit until the sauce is thickened. Adjust the seasoning. ·

Dried rabbit: Dry leftover braised or stewed rabbit in a food dehydrator until all of the moisture has been removed. Or place the rabbit on a large screen over a baking sheet, and dry in the oven on the lowest setting. Turn the rabbit occasionally, until the meat is very dry. Shred and then store in a covered container for a week.

Dried rabbit

BISON

Bison were always present when I was growing up. We'd ride our bikes over the prairies and pass by herds whose mammoth size was enough to scare anyone. The truth is, though, they're mild-mannered animals, gentle and shy. Buffalo are iconic figures in Native stories, legends, and paintings. They inspire costumes at powwows and ceremonies. When we were very young, we were told stories of how the Creator gave bison to the Lakota people so we wouldn't starve. Before I left Pine Ridge, the bison were beginning to return to the land, reintroduced by the National Park Service and a few local ranches.

"The bison is symbolic of the relationship we have to the earth and to each other," Joseph Marshall, Native American poet and historian, told me. "This animal has kept us alive for generations, providing us with food, clothing, medicine, and tools. The Sundance is how we honor the bison and continue to do so today."

BISON MEAT

Some older people say bison reminds them of the beef they ate when they were young. It's leaner; it's lighter yet richer tasting, delicious but easy to overcook. The best rule of thumb is to cook it low and slow *or* high and fast. Bison meat is high in protein, low in fat and cholesterol, and grass-fed bison meat is a good source of omega-3 fatty acids.

If bison is not available, grass-fed beef may be substituted for bison in all recipes.

BISON TARTARE

Pté Tȟaló Špáŋšniyaŋ
Serves 4 to 6

Bison Tartare, duck egg yolk, Amaranth Cracker

Bison is the cleanest-tasting red meat, milder and a little sweeter than beef. Tartare showcases this clean taste. Here it's seasoned with juniper and mint and gets a tangy kick from sumac.

8 ounces boneless bison, trimmed of fat and silver skin, finely chopped

1 tablespoon crushed juniper

1 tablespoon chopped mint

2 teaspoons maple sugar

1 tablespoon finely chopped wild onion or shallots

1 tablespoon sumac

1 teaspoon sunflower oil

Salt

In a medium bowl, combine the chopped bison, juniper, mint, maple sugar, onion, sumac, and oil. Season with the salt. Form into patties and serve topped with a duck egg yolk and cracker of your choice.

BISON RIBS

Ťhathúčhuhu
Serves 4 to 6

Bison Ribs, braised greens, griddled apples

Finger-licking, rib-sucking, and tasty, these ribs are lean, crispy, and tender.

1 tablespoon ground juniper
1 tablespoon salt
1 teaspoon ground sage
4 to 6 pounds bison ribs
1 cup water
½ cup Wojape, page 173

Preheat the broiler or grill to high. In a small bowl, combine the juniper, salt, and sage and rub over the ribs to season. Grill both sides of the ribs under the broiler or on the grill until a firm crust forms, about 2 to 3 minutes per side. Reduce oven tempreature to 250°F.

Place the ribs bone side down on a rack and set in a roasting pan; alternatively, set the rack on a deep baking sheet. Add a cup of water to the pan. Cover or wrap tightly with foil and roast for 2 hours. Turn the ribs over, cover, and continue roasting until the meat is very tender, about 45 minutes to 1 hour.

Remove the ribs and scoop about ¼ cup of the pan juices into a small bowl and whisk in the Wojape. Brush the ribs with the Wojape sauce and return to the grill or run under the broiler to glaze the meat, about 3 to 5 minutes. Remove the ribs to a cutting board, allow them to rest a few minutes, then cut into serving pieces and serve with additional Wojape.

THE NOBLE WAY TO HUNT

"As you hunt, you bond with the animals and you start to match heartbeats," my uncle Richard Sherman told me. "When you do that, respect for them and the land comes naturally. You realize whatever you do has an impact . . . For me, it's important to follow the noble way to kill an animal cleanly with one shot, so that it just drops straight down. You can't do this until you learn to know the animals." He's a wildlife biologist, coauthor of *Collaborative Stewardship of Nature: Knowledge Binds and Institutional Conflicts,* who grew up hunting as a means of providing food for his siblings. A tough, smart man, he was one of my role models and he instilled in me the values that have guided me in my work.

Now retired, Uncle Richard lives in Rapid City, South Dakota, where he's working on another book and gives tours of the Pine Ridge Reservation. He often guides visitors to the magnificent places near his ancestral home so they can experience the power of the land.

CEDAR-BRAISED BISON

Ȟaŋté úŋ Pté Lolóbyapi
Serves 6 to 8

This makes a simple and hearty one-pot meal. The meat becomes fork tender and the stock simmers down to a rich sauce. Leftovers are terrific served over corn cakes.

When braising meat, we always add a handful of the ingredients we intend to serve alongside—such as hominy, wild rice, and dried berries. You need to soak the dried hominy overnight before adding, so be sure to plan ahead.

BRAISING, AN ANCIENT METHOD

Braising meat in a flavorful stock over low heat for a long time is our preferred way of cooking large game because it's so lean and dries out easily. The cooking liquids along with the herbs and spices infuse the meat with flavor. Once it's fork tender, we brown the meat under the broiler or over a flame. We then simmer the cooking liquid to reduce it into a lush, thick sauce.

We always add the ingredients for the side dish to the braising liquid. We may add wild rice, soaked hominy, or squash to the Cedar-Braised Bison. They add subtle flavors that bring together the final dish.

2 to 3 pounds bison or beef chuck roast

1 tablespoon coarse salt

2 tablespoons maple sugar

3 tablespoons sunflower oil

2 to 4 cups Wild Rice or Corn Stock, page 170

Several sprigs sage

1 sprig cedar

2 cups dried hominy, soaked overnight and drained

1 tablespoon sumac

½ cup maple syrup

Preheat the oven to 250°F. Season the bison with the salt and maple sugar. Film a Dutch oven or large flame-proof baking dish with the oil and set over high heat. Sear the bison on all sides until dark and crusty, about 10 minutes. Remove the bison and set aside. Stir in the stock and sage, scraping up any of the crusty bits that form on the bottom of the baking dish. Add the hominy, sumac, and maple syrup and return the meat to the baking dish. Cover the Dutch oven or the baking dish tightly. (Use aluminum foil, if necessary.) Place the bison in the oven and cook until so tender it falls from the bone, about 3 hours.

Remove from the oven. Tent the meat with foil to keep warm. Strain the remaining stock into a saucepan and reserve the hominy. Set the stock over high heat, bring to a boil, and reduce the liquid by half. Taste and adjust the seasoning. Carve the bison and serve over the hominy with the sauce drizzled over the meat.

INDIGENOUS TACOS

Ikčé Wičháša Ağúyapi Oštéka

Serves 6 to 8

When we launched the Tatanka Truck, we took the idea of the fast food—Indian Tacos—and slowed it down with authentic ingredients. This is a delicious and superhealthy alternative to the fry bread and commodity hamburger version. Use leftover Cedar-Braised Bison, page 120, or Cedar-Braised Beans, page 36, or Griddled Maple Squash, page 33, in lieu of the ground bison in this recipe. The recipe is easily expanded to feed a crowd.

2 to 3 pounds ground bison

Generous pinch salt

Generous pinch juniper

2 tablespoons sunflower oil

4 wild onions or 2 medium onions, chopped

1 tablespoon chopped sage leaves

½ cup Corn or Wild Rice Stock, page 170

1 to 2 tablespoons maple syrup to taste

Corn Cakes, page 51

Wojape, page 173

Corn Nuts, page 176

Chopped sorrel for garnish (optional)

Season the bison with the salt and juniper. Heat the sunflower oil in a large Dutch oven over high heat and add the onions. Cook until softened and lightly browned, about 3 to 4 minutes. Add the bison and sage, and cook until browned, about 3 to 4 minutes, stirring occasionally to break up the meat. Add the stock, bring to a simmer, and cook until the liquid is reduced to a glaze, about 3 minutes. Season with the maple syrup. Serve over the corn cakes and drizzle with Wojape. Garnish with sorrel and top with corn nuts for a nice crunch.

Chef's Note: For vegetarian and vegan tacos, replace the bison with Cedar-Braised Beans, page 36.

Indigenous Tacos

TANKA

Native American Natural Foods, LLC, Pine Ridge Reservation, South Dakota, produces buffalo-based packaged foods that are delicious, nutritious, healthy, and sustainable. The company's mission is to support the region's natural buffalo herd, employ members of the tribe, and contribute to the local economy. The Tanka Bar, made with buffalo, dried fruit, and natural seasonings, is wildly popular. It contains no artificial ingredients and is low-carbohydrate, sugar free, and gluten free. In a pinch, we substitute these products for Wasna, page 125.

The mission of the company, founded by Karlene Hunter and Mark Tilsen in 2006, is to produce foods that add to the restoration and preservation of our lands and the ecosystem. Because they are made with natural, healthful ingredients, they may help to reverse chronic food-related illnesses such as obesity and diabetes. These are foods that align with the ways Native Americans lived just a century ago. "Tanka" speaks to the ability to "Live Life Powerfully and to acknowledge 'Mitakuye Oyasin'—we are all related."

BISON WASNA

Pté Wasná
Makes about 10 to 12 ounces

Wasna, or dried meats, are as delicious and versatile as they are ancient, and they are exceptionally easy to make. We use wasna in salads, on top of wild rice and hominy cakes as an appetizer, and in soups and stews, for they have an extraordinary flavor. Wasna is sometimes called pemmican—the mix of dried meat and berries. It's rough, sweet, and immensely nutritious and satisfying—loaded with protein, low in sugar and carbs—the original good-for-you snack food.

Serve the wasna cakes on a "charcuterie" board with Smoked Pheasant, page 106, dried berries, toasted hazelnuts, seeds, greens, and a little crock of Wojape, page 173.

2 pounds bison, flank, rump, or round
2 teaspoons crushed juniper
½ cup dried cranberries
Pinch coarse salt

Trim the meat of fat, place in a freezer bag, and put into the freezer for about an hour or until very firm (this makes it much easier to slice).

Remove the meat and slice thinly with the grain into long strips. Put the strips, along with the remaining ingredients, back into the freezer bag and refrigerate at least 3 hours or overnight.

Preheat the oven to 150°F. Or prepare a dehydrator. Remove the meat from the bag and pat dry. Arrange the strips on a food dehydrator or a screen or drying rack placed over a baking sheet to catch any drips. If using a screen, place in the oven. Allow the meat to dry until it is leathery, at least 4 hours or overnight. Remove, cool, and cut into bite-sized pieces.

Put the meat and the cranberries into a food processor fitted with a steel blade. Pulse and season with the salt. Remove and shape into small cakes.

Bison Wasna

HUNTER'S STEW

Wóle Wičháša Wahánpi Tȟáwa

Serves 4 to 6

Bear remains a traditional Native food, especially in the Northern Heartland, where these animals are abundant. They're known to raid summer cabins and park dumpsters, and to snatch small pets. Hunting bear for food is one of the best ways to control the expanding population.

Moose, elk, and antelope are also great choices for this recipe because the slow cooking helps to turn the meat tender and flavorful. If these are not available, substitute bison or lamb. Serve it over Corn Cakes, page 51, or Cornmeal Mush, page 59, or with Kneel Down Bread, page 55. Like most hearty stews, it will taste better the day after it's made.

1 ounce dried wild mushrooms, such as chanterelles, trumpet, or morels

1 cup boiling water

3 tablespoons sunflower oil

2½ to 3 pounds bear, lamb, or bison, cut into 2-inch cubes

Coarse salt

Crushed juniper

3 wild onions or 1 large leek, white part, trimmed

8 ounces fresh mushrooms, coarsely chopped

1 tablespoon minced fresh oregano

2 teaspoons sumac to taste

1 cup Corn or Bison Stock, page 170

Put the dried mushrooms in a small bowl and pour the boiling water over them. Soak about 20 minutes until softened. Drain and reserve the soaking liquid. Chop the mushrooms and set aside.

In a large, heavy pot, heat the sunflower oil over medium-high heat and brown the meat pieces in batches, seasoning with salt and juniper. Be careful not to crowd the pan. Cook each batch about 10 to 15 minutes. Remove the browned meat to a platter.

Reduce the heat and add the onions, mushrooms, oregano, and sumac, and sauté until the onion is soft and the mushrooms release some of their liquid, about 3 to 5 minutes. Stir in the chopped, reconstituted wild mushrooms and the soaking liquid and the stock, stirring to dislodge any brown bits that stick to the pan.

Return the meat to the pot, bring to a simmer, and cook, partially covered, until the meat is fork tender, about 2 hours. Taste and adjust the seasonings. Remove from the heat and let sit a few minutes before serving.

Hunter's Stew, mashed squash, cranberries

GRILLED BISON SKEWERS WITH WOJAPE
Serves 4 to 6

Everyone loves these kebobs, the recipe of Mikee Willard and his son Darius Willard of the Northern Cheyenne tribe in Montana, and members of the Tatanka Truck team. They skewer chunks of fresh sweet corn (on the cob), turnips, summer squash, or partially roasted winter squash in between the bison. The skewers are then garnished with Wojape, page 173, or a sauce of stewed wild plums.

1 to 1½ pounds bison sirloin, cut into 1- to 2-inch cubes
2 tablespoons sunflower oil
Pinch sumac
Pinch smoked salt
2 to 3 ears of sweet corn, shucked and cut into 2-inch chunks
2 to 4 young turnips, cut into 2-inch chunks
3 summer squash, cut into 2-inch chunks

Heat coals or a gas grill for direct heat. Brush the bison with 1 tablespoon of the sunflower oil and sprinkle with the sumac and smoked salt. Brush the corn, turnips, and squash with the remaining oil. Thread the meat, sweet corn, turnips, and squash alternately on 4 to 6 skewers. Sprinkle the meat and vegetables with additional sumac and smoked salt.

Grill the skewers about 4 to 6 inches from the heat, turning frequently, until the bison is no longer pink in the center, about 15 to 20 minutes. Serve drizzled with the Wojape, page 173.

TANIGA

Taniga is a traditional soup made of tripe reserved for feasts and ceremonies. It's tricky to make, requiring hours of soaking the bison intestines to be sure they are clean, before simmering in a broth with timpsula and onions. The elders always looked forward to taniga, but I don't remember any of us kids ever being excited to dig in. But we understood that the food was important because it made use of the entire buffalo, a sacred animal. Once the bison was slaughtered, none of it ever went to waste.

Taniga is made for special occasions, similar to Mexican *menudo* soup, German *Kuttelsuppe,* French *tripes à la mode de Caen,* and Polish *flaki.*

LAMB SAUSAGE

Tȟáčhiŋčala Tȟašúpa
Makes about 3 pounds

Brian Yazzie, Sioux Chef chef de cuisine, shared his method for creating a traditional Diné lamb sausage. Churro lamb, introduced to the continent by Spanish explorers in the 1600s, has become a mainstay throughout the Southwest. It's an especially hardy animal, requiring less water and forage than other sheep, with long legs, a narrow body, and fine bones. Navajo-Churro sheep provide lean meat with a distinctive, sweet flavor and beautiful dual-fiber fleece, prized for its array of natural colors and woven into Navajo tapestries and blankets.

The breed was nearly brought to extinction in the 1860s when the U.S. government declared the Navajo enemies and rounded up the Diné people, destroyed their livestock, burned orchards and crops, and forced them onto the four-hundred-mile "Long Walk" into New Mexico. Today, the Navajo-Churro is considered a heritage breed, raised throughout the United States and Canada.

Because the traditional recipe for Churro lamb sausage is the kind of food best learned at the side of an elder, we've modified it, using more readily available ingredients. (The original recipe for this traditional blood sausage is similar to British black pudding, French boudin, and Estonian Christmas pudding—all truly delicious.)

Brown this off to serve in our Indigenous Tacos, page 122, or in a Fried Wild Rice Bowl, page 83. Shape into patties for the grill.

3 pounds boneless lamb shoulder, or combination of cuts, cut into 1-inch cubes
¼ cup water
2 tablespoons maple vinegar
2 teaspoons coarse salt
2 teaspoons chopped sage
2 teaspoons chopped oregano
Generous pinch sumac
Generous pinch crushed juniper

Place the lamb on a rimmed baking sheet, transfer to the freezer, and chill until it's stiff but not frozen.

Grind the meat through the small die of a meat grinder into a bowl. Work the water, vinegar, salt, sage, oregano, sumac, and juniper into the meat. To check the flavor of the sausage, cook a little of it in a lightly greased skillet set over medium-high heat until lightly browned; then taste and adjust the seasonings. Store the sausage covered in the refrigerator or freeze.

VENISON CHOPS WITH APPLES AND CRANBERRIES

Tȟáȟča nakúŋ Tȟaspáŋ na Watȟókeča T'áǧa

Serves 4

Here the venison chops are cooked quickly over high heat to be especially tender and juicy.

2 tart apples*
1 cup cider
¼ cup maple syrup
4 cups cranberries
8 3- to 4-ounce venison rib chops or rack of venison cut into 8 chops**
Salt
Crushed juniper
2 tablespoons sunflower oil

Put the apples, cider, maple syrup, and cranberries into a small, heavy saucepan. Set over high heat and bring to a boil. Reduce the heat and simmer until the liquid is reduced to ¼ cup, about 10 to 12 minutes. Remove and set aside.

Preheat the oven to 500°F. Rinse and pat the chops dry and season with the salt and juniper. Heat the sunflower oil in a heavy skillet and set over moderate to high heat. Sauté the chops in batches, turning once, until well browned, about 2 minutes per side, 4 minutes total. Transfer the chops to a shallow baking pan and roast in the preheated oven until medium rare, about 3 minutes. Serve the chops with the cooked apples and cranberries.

*We prefer using wild crabapples for their tartness, but if those are unavailable, substitute tart, domestic apples such as greening, Haralson, or Keepsake.

**If venison isn't available, pork may be substituted.

VENISON OR ELK STEW WITH HOMINY

Tȟáȟča naíŋš Heȟáka na Pašláyapi Waháŋpi

Serves 4 to 6

Venison shoulder is perfect for this recipe. The meat is lean and the muscles break down to become silky and tender during the slow braise. If you can't find shoulder, use shanks. They'll need to cook a little longer but are equally delicious.

This is great served with hominy, over Old-fashioned Cornmeal Mush, page 59, or roasted squash.

1 4-pound venison or elk shoulder*
Pinch smoked salt
Pinch crushed juniper
2 tablespoons sunflower oil
2 wild onions or small shallots, diced
1 pound wild mushrooms (chanterelle, oyster, porcini, or cremini), sliced
¼ cup corn flour
3 cups Corn Stock, page 170, or vegetable stock
1 cup cider, hard or not sweet
1 sprig sage
1 to 2 tablespoons maple vinegar to taste
Dash maple sugar

Generously season all sides of the venison with the salt and juniper. Film a cast-iron pot with the oil and set over high heat. Add the venison and sear well on all sides until golden brown, about 4 minutes per side. Remove the venison and set aside.

Reduce the heat and add the onions and mushrooms to the pot and cook, stirring until they brown, about 3 to 4 minutes. Stir in the flour until dissolved; then stir in the stock, cider, and sage and bring the mixture to a boil. Reduce the heat to a low simmer. Cover and cook until the meat pulls away easily from the bone, about 1½ to 2 hours. Taste and season with the vinegar and sugar.

Transfer the venison to a cutting board and remove the bone. Slice the meat into chunks and return to the pot. Discard the sprig of sage. Serve in shallow bowls over wild rice, corn cakes, hominy, or roasted squash.

* If venison is not available, substitute lamb or goat in this recipe.

NATURE'S SWEETS, TEAS, AND REFRESHING DRINKS

Creating delicious desserts without wheat flour, dairy, or processed sugar—the holy trinity of treats—may sound daunting. But in rebuilding this food system literally from the ground up, we've let our imaginations roam outside of the European dessert box. Nature's sweet gifts are the focus here.

These recipes rely on sweet and tangy fruits, corn and squash (roasted to caramelize their sugars), tree sap, honey, agave, and fruit syrups. The first people didn't use much honey, but it plays a significant role in our kitchen. We enjoy its natural goodness and versatility. Bees are pollinators, vital to our local food system, and we believe apiaries should be a part of every community.

Dessert at the end of a meal is a European convention. Our ancestors relied on sweet foods for energy; they played an important role in a healthy diet and were not considered indulgences. Chocolate was enjoyed as a bitter or savory drink until the Spanish arrived and sweetened it up. We've included a few recipes for chocolate sweetened with agave, because these two ingredients come from the same region. We also provide recipes for the traditional seed cakes our warriors, farmers, and foragers once carried with them as snacks.

Our refreshing teas and drinks pair beautifully with our meals. Some are calming, others are energizing; we enjoy them throughout the day. It was common for tribes to have drinking water with berries, herbs, or other flavors steeping in the camp. Food is medicine, and as we rediscover these delicious, nutritious, healing foods, we are reconnecting with our past and revitalizing our culture.

Sunflower Cookies

SUNFLOWER COOKIES

Waȟčázi Tȟáŋka Sú Aǧúyabskuyela

Makes about 1 dozen cookies

Our signature sweet, sunflower cookies are delicious any time of day and are inspired by the sunflower cakes Native warriors relied on for strength and endurance. Sunflower is packed with magnesium, B vitamins, and protein—all extremely beneficial to girls and women.

1 cup Sunny Butter, page 166

¼ cup maple syrup or honey to taste

Pinch salt

¼ cup cornmeal

Preheat the oven to 350°F. In a small bowl, stir together the Sunny Butter, maple syrup, and salt, adding a little warm water if the dough is too stiff. Using a tablespoon, scoop up balls of the mixture and roll in the cornmeal. Place on a cookie sheet and flatten slightly with your hand. Bake the cookies until just firm, about 8 to 10 minutes. Remove and set on a rack to cool.

EDIBLE FLOWERS

The flowers of berry bushes and fruit trees are beautiful garnishes and make a light, sweet addition to salads and sautés. Don't pick too many or the plant won't bear fruit. One or two won't make much difference to the harvest, but it will light up the plate. Scatter the edible flowers over sorbets or sweet cookies or cakes.

AUTUMN HARVEST COOKIES

Ptaŋyétu Wóksapi Aǧúyabskuyela

Makes about 12 cookies

These cookies are not at all sweet. Their flavor will depend on the flour you choose to use. Or try a combination of flours for power-packed, distinctive cookies.

½ cup vegetable, Wild Rice, Chestnut, or Acorn Meal Flour, pages 167, 169

½ cup fine cornmeal or corn flour

¼ cup Sunny Butter, page 166

Generous pinch salt

¼ cup maple sugar or 3 tablespoons honey

2 tablespoons sunflower or walnut oil

¼ cup dried cranberries, cooked wild rice, or chopped nuts

Preheat the oven to 350°F. In a large mixing bowl, whisk together the flour (or flours), Sunny Butter, and salt. Stir in the maple sugar or honey, oil, and any of the other ingredients to make a stiff dough. Line a cookie sheet with parchment paper or a silicone mat. Use a teaspoon and your hands to form 1-inch balls and place them about 1 inch apart on the baking sheet. Flatten slightly with your fingers. Bake until the cookies are slightly firm and browned at the edges, about 8 to 10 minutes. Enjoy warm or cool and store in an airtight container for about 3 days.

Autumn Harvest Cookies, berry sorbet

CORN COOKIES

Wagmíza Ağúyabskuyela
Makes 12 small cookies

Sweetened with maple sugar and glazed with maple syrup, these crisp cookies are delicious with cedar tea. They will keep a week in a covered container.

¼ cup Sunny Butter, page 166
3 tablespoons sunflower or hazelnut oil
¼ cup maple sugar
1 cup fine cornmeal or corn flour
Maple sugar for dusting

Preheat the oven to 350°F. Lightly grease a cooking sheet or griddle. In a large bowl, mix together the Sunny Butter, oil, maple sugar, and cornmeal or corn flour. Using a teaspoon, drop generous portions of dough on the baking sheet and lightly flatten with your fingers. Bake until the dough is firm, about 10 to 15 minutes. Remove and cool. Store in an airtight container.

AMARANTH BITES

Waȟpé Yatȟápi Iyéčheča Ağúyabskuyela

Makes 12 cookies

Amaranth Bites with Raspberry–Rose Hip Sauce

Fill these soft, rich cookies with the Raspberry–Rose-Hip Sauce or your favorite jam.

2 cups dough for Amaranth Crackers, page 60
¼ cup maple sugar
Pinch salt
Raspberry–Rose-Hip Sauce, page 142 (optional)

Preheat the oven to 350°F. Line a cookie sheet with parchment paper. In a medium bowl, stir together the amaranth dough and the sugar. Using a teaspoon, scoop out small balls of the dough and arrange about 1 inch apart on the parchment. If filling the cookie, make an indent in the center with your thumb. Bake until slightly golden and firm, about 5 to 8 minutes. Serve with a dollop of Raspberry–Rose-Hip Sauce or your favorite jam, or sprinkle with additional maple sugar.

CHOCOLATE PECAN BITES

Makes about 12 to 14 small bites

It's hard to deny the allure of chocolate, the gift of the ancient Aztecs to the Spanish. Chocolate was first enjoyed as a dark, bitter beverage, and sugar was introduced later on. Here we've blended cocoa butter, raw cocoa powder, and pecans with a little agave as a sweetener. Although none of these ingredients are native to our region, they represent the ways we can all share in the joys of indigenous flavors throughout the Americas.

½ cup cocoa butter
½ cup raw cocoa powder
2 cups pecans, lightly toasted
Pinch salt
½ vanilla bean
3 tablespoons agave to taste

Line a small tray or flat plate with parchment paper. In a small saucepan set over low heat, melt the cocoa butter. Stir in the cocoa powder and set aside.

In a food processor fitted with a steel blade, grind the pecans into a paste, stopping occasionally to scrape down the sides. Slowly add the cocoa butter mixture, salt, the seeds of the vanilla bean, and agave until smooth.

Transfer the mixture to a bowl and, using a teaspoon, shape small balls or bites and set on the parchment-lined tray. Put into the refrigerator until set. Serve at room temperature.

CHESTNUTS

Until the early 1900s, American chestnut trees filled our forests from Georgia to Canada, stretching west through Ohio to southern Wisconsin, Minnesota, and Iowa. One out of every four hardwood trees was a chestnut. In the forests, where trees compete for sunlight and nutrients, some chestnuts grew larger in diameter than a dining-room table and as high as a seven-story building. They came into flower in late June, making the rolling hills they favor appear to be buried in snow.

Nicknamed the "bread tree," the chestnut tree provided a staple that could be boiled and mashed like potatoes and dried and ground into flour to make bread. Chestnuts were eaten out of hand, raw, or roasted as a satisfying and nutritious snack, and the leaves were made into a tea as a traditional method for treating whooping cough. In October, the vast stands provided a limitless supply of food, dropping nuts that glistened like gems and fed people, wild turkeys, geese, and other game.

All of this came to an end around the turn of the twentieth century when exotic and unusual species became the fashion in formal gardens of mansions across the East Coast. Plant hobbyists introduced Asian chestnut trees and inadvertently imported a fungus. By 1904, scientists discovered that this same fungus caused cankers on New York City's American chestnut trees. The Asian trees are resistant to the fungus, but on the American species, the cankers cut off the tree's ability to transport water and nutrients and quickly "strangled" the trees to death. The fungus that causes the blight lives in the bark of other trees, such as oak and ash, without killing them. Carried by the wind, birds, and animals, the fungus spread swiftly and the blight raced through forests at up to fifty miles a year. Lumber companies assumed that the chestnut tree's end was inevitable and so clear-cut forests for the valuable timber. Hybrid chestnut trees are beginning to replace the lost mighty chestnut, reforesting damaged land and providing us with chestnuts once more.

RASPBERRY–ROSE-HIP SAUCE

Tȟakhánheča na Uŋžíŋžiŋtka Iyúltȟuŋ

Makes ¾ cup

Use this bright, tangy sauce on meats or in vinaigrettes. Sweetened with maple syrup or honey, it makes a lovely drizzle on sweet Corn Cakes, page 51, or Wild Rice Cakes, page 63, or drizzled over any of the sorbets, pages 147–49.

1 cup raspberries
½ cup fresh rose hips or ¼ cup dried rose hips
½ cup water or more as needed
Splash maple syrup

Combine the raspberries, rose hips, and water in a small saucepan and set over medium heat. Bring to a simmer and cook until the raspberries have collapsed and the rose hips are soft. Strain through a fine-mesh strainer, pressing out as much of the pulp as possible. Sweeten to taste with the maple syrup.

ACORN AND WILD RICE CAKES

Úta na psíŋ pakpáŋ kčeyápi
Serves 8

These dark, moist, dense cakes, created by Tashia Hart, our culinary ethnobotanist and a member of the Red Lake Band of Chippewa, are a winning dessert. Tashia's talent for identifying and using wild edibles enhances our menus. She has an eye for beauty and flavor as well as a keen understanding of the earth's gifts.

Tashia serves these cakes with a sauce of sweetened, reduced chaga and Wild Rice Pudding, page 145, with currant sauce.

1 cup Acorn Meal Flour, page 169
½ cup Wild Rice Flour, page 167
¼ cup sunflower oil, or more as needed
¼ cup honey
Pinch salt

Preheat the oven to 350°F. Line a baking sheet with parchment paper. In a medium bowl, whisk together the flours and then stir in the oil and honey to make a smooth dough. Season with a little salt. Using a tablespoon, scoop out the dough onto the parchment and pat into rounds. Bake until the cakes are firm, about 12 to 15 minutes. Remove and cool.

POPPED AMARANTH CAKES (*ALEGRÍA*)

Waȟpé Yatȟápi Iyéčheča Nabláȟyapi

Makes 2 cups

Alegría means joy in Spanish, and these sweets are traditional in Oaxaca, Mexico. Although most recipes call for *piloncillo,* a processed form of brown cane sugar, maple syrup or honey works well. The recipe is simple and straightforward, and the results are delicious and healthful.

½ cup amaranth
¼ cup sunflower seeds
¼ cup dried cranberries or blueberries (optional)
½ cup maple syrup or honey

Line a cutting board or baking sheet with parchment paper. Heat a skillet or wok over a high flame and add a tablespoon of amaranth. Stir lightly to keep from burning; the grain will start popping in about 30 seconds. Transfer to a bowl. Continue popping the amaranth a tablespoon at a time until it has all popped. Stir the sunflower seeds and dried fruit, if using, into the amaranth.

In a small pot, bring the maple syrup or honey to a full boil to thicken and when it is reduced by half, about 7 minutes, add to the popped grain. Mound the amaranth onto the prepared board or baking sheet. Using a rolling pin, gently shape it into a square or rectangle about ½ inch thick. When just cool enough to handle, cut into squares with a sharp knife dipped in cold water. Store in an airtight container with parchment paper between the layers of bars.

WILD RICE PUDDING

Psíŋ Yužápi
Serves 4 to 6

This pudding is delicious for breakfast as well as a snack. Cook the wild rice down even further to become firm and then shape into patties to brown in a frying pan as pancakes.

4 cups cooked wild rice
3 cups Sunflower or Hazelnut Milk, 146, 148
Salt to taste
Maple sugar to taste

In a large pot, simmer the cooked wild rice in the nut milk until very soft, about 15 minutes. Add 2 cups of the wild rice to a food processor fitted with a steel blade and puree. Return to the pot and stir to combine. Season with maple syrup, honey, or Wojape, page 173, and toasted nuts. Serve warm.

Wild Rice Cakes Variation: To make wild rice cakes, continue cooking the wild rice mixture until very sticky. Cool, then shape into patties. Film a heavy skillet with sunflower or hazelnut oil and set over medium-high heat. Sear the patties until browned on both sides, about 3 to 4 minutes per side.

RICING MOON

The Ojibwe Ricing Moon, *manoominike-giizis,* is the season of the harvest, a ceremony, and a way of life. "You get to visit people you haven't seen for a whole year, because just about everyone goes ricing," says Spud Fineday of White Earth. To this day, the harvest is celebrated with feasts of thanksgiving. "The complex traditions associated with food production embody a rich understanding of the environment, including all aspects of traditional ecological knowledge, from practical strategies and management techniques, to belief systems that guide sustainable use of resources, to ways of communicating and acquiring knowledge," notes Nancy Turner in *Ancient Pathways, Ancestral Knowledge: Ethnobotany and Ecological Wisdom of Indigenous Peoples of Northwestern North America,*one of her many books.

SUNFLOWER MILK SORBET

Waȟčázi Tȟáŋka Čhaȟsníyaŋ
Makes 1 cup

Nut milks make a delicious alternative to dairy. Sunflower milk is a cinch to make and is the basis for this delicious sorbet. Serve it topped with berries or caramelized sunflower seeds. It's a sweet, light, and refreshing end to a meal.

1 cup sunflower seeds
3 cups water
¼ cup maple syrup
Pinch salt

Soak the sunflower seeds in the water overnight. Then pulse the seeds and water, maple syrup, and a pinch of salt in a blender until the seeds are pulverized, about 3 to 5 minutes. Taste and adjust the sweetening. For a rich sorbet, place this mixture in an ice-cream maker or a 9 x 13–inch cake pan. For a lighter sorbet, strain the milk through a strainer lined with cheesecloth, pressing out all of the liquid into a 9 x 13–inch cake pan or ice-cream maker and discard the pulp. Put in the freezer. When the sorbet is frozen, cut it into chunks and process it in a food processor fitted with a steel blade until it is smooth and creamy. Serve immediately.

SUNFLOWERS

Sunflowers are among the first flowers planted in the spring and the last to be harvested in the fall. When heavy and full, the heads were collected in baskets and dried, facedown. Sunflower seeds were pounded into flour and butter and used to thicken soups and stews or to shape into patties and cakes. Sunflower butter, like peanut butter, is rich and creamy, slightly sweet, delicious as a spread, and tasty in cookies and sweets. Sunflower sprouts and young leaves are delicious mixed with salad greens. The larger leaves make fine vessels for cooking.

If you grow your own sunflowers, the flowers will tell you when the seeds are ready to harvest. The heads will be droopy and the center petals will be dry and the seeds clearly visible. To harvest, cut the flower's head from the stalk and place it facedown on a flat surface. Rub the center to shake the seeds from the flower.

SWEET CORN SORBET

Waštúŋkala Čhaŋsníyaŋ

Servest 4 to 6

Sweet Corn Sorbet with Native Granola Bars

Sweet corn milk is the essence of this lush dessert that's actually more like ice cream, though it contains no cream, milk, or eggs. Serve garnished with chopped mint and/or fresh berries. Nuts and berries are always a great addition to any sorbet!

4 to 6 ears of very fresh sweet corn
¼ cup maple syrup, or to taste
Pinch salt

Shuck the corn. One by one, stand each ear on its flat end in a shallow bowl and, using a sharp knife, slice the kernels into the bowl. Scrape the cobs with the dull edge of the knife to capture the milky liquid as well. Place the kernels, milky liquid, and the cobs into a wide saucepan and add just enough water to cover. Bring to a boil. Reduce the heat and cook until the kernels are just tender, about 3 to 5 minutes. Remove and discard the cobs. Scoop out the kernels with a strainer and transfer to a blender. Add the maple syrup and puree the kernels, adding equal parts of the milky liquid as needed, to create a thick slurry. Season with a little salt. Transfer the mixture to an ice-cream maker or large baking dish and freeze.

Roasted Sweet Corn Variation: Pan-roast the corn kernels in a dry skillet or under the broiler before continuing with the recipe. This will sweeten them slightly and add an extra golden color to the sorbet. Alternatively, fold toasted corn kernels into the sorbet before putting it into the freezer.

HAZELNUT MAPLE SORBET

Úma na Čhaŋháŋpi Tiktíča Čhaȟsníyaŋ

Serves 4 to 6

Hazelnut Maple Sorbet, dried apple slice, Autumn Harvest Cookie

Hazelnut milk is simple to make, but if you're short on time, feel free to use the organic packaged milk now available in many natural food co-ops and supermarkets.

3 cups hazelnuts
4 cups water, divided
½ cup maple syrup to taste
Pinch salt to taste

Preheat the oven to 350°F. Put the hazelnuts on a roasting pan and bake in the oven until they smell nutty and the skins crack, about 10 to 15 minutes. Remove, place in a clean dish towel, and rub to remove some of the skins.

Put the hazelnuts into a jar and cover with water. Soak for at least 2 hours or overnight. Strain the hazelnuts. Rinse and put into a blender with 2 cups of fresh water. Blend until smooth and creamy. Strain through a nut milk bag or cheesecloth until most of the liquid is removed.

Pour the nut milk into a bowl and add the maple syrup and salt to taste. Transfer to an ice-cream maker or large baking dish and freeze. Temper slightly at room temperature before serving.

WILD RICE SORBET

Psíŋ Čhaȟsníyaŋ

Serves 4 to 6

This surprisingly creamy sorbet is wonderful topped with blueberries, raspberries, or sweetened cranberries. Remove it from the freezer to temper before serving.

2 cups Wild Rice Stock, page 170
1 cup well-cooked wild rice
3 to 4 tablespoons maple sugar
Pinch salt
Puffed Wild Rice, page 175, for garnish (optional)

In a food processor fitted with a steel blade or in a blender, puree the stock, wild rice, maple sugar, and salt. Place into an ice-cream maker or a shallow baking dish and freeze, stirring occasionally, until semifrozen. Serve garnished with the popped wild rice, if desired.

MAPLE SQUASH SORBET WITH CRANBERRY SAUCE

Čhaŋháŋpi Tiktíča na Wagmú Čhaȟsníyaŋ nakúŋ Watȟókeča T'áǧa Yužápi

Serves 4 to 6

This sorbet has plenty of body, yet is light and fresh-tasting. People are always surprised by how creamy and unctuous it tastes, but you won't leave the table feeling weighed down.

2 pounds butternut squash
1¼ cups maple syrup
¼ cup cider
Cranberry Sauce, page 108

Preheat the oven to 325°F. Cut the squash in half lengthwise, remove the seeds, and place on a baking tray, cut side down. Add a little water to the tray and bake until the squash is fork tender, about 1 hour. Remove from the oven. When cool enough to handle, scoop out the flesh and place in a blender or food processor fitted with a steel blade. Add the maple syrup and cider and puree. Transfer into an ice-cream maker or a shallow baking dish and freeze, stirring occasionally. Serve the Cranberry Sauce over the sorbet.

BLUEBERRY–RASPBERRY–BERGAMOT SPOON SWEET

Háza na Tȟakȟáŋheča na Waȟpé Waštémna Yužápi
Makes 2 pints

This bright jam doubles as a sauce or a "spoon sweet" to serve on top of cookies, spread over cakes, or dolloped onto Wild Rice Pudding, page 145, or Sweet Corn Sorbet, page 147.

4 cups mixed blueberries and raspberries
2 to 3 tablespoons chopped bergamot leaves
¼ cup maple sugar or honey to taste

Put all of the ingredients into a medium saucepan set over medium-low heat. Press the berries to release their juices; cover and bring to a low simmer. Remove the lid and simmer until the mixture is thick enough to coat the back of a spoon. Remove from the heat. Cool and store in a covered container in the refrigerator. This will keep about a week.

WILD APPLE SAUCE (SAVORY OR SWEET)

Ťhaspáŋ Yužápi

Makes about 2 to 3 pints

This simple sauce can be made savory or sweet, depending on the ingredients. It's great with game birds when spiced with cedar and/or sage for a savory sauce. Add a little mint and honey or late-season blueberries, and you have a fine sweet.

3 pounds wild apples or a mix of domestic and crab apples, cored and coarsely chopped
¼ cup cider
Pinch salt
2 tablespoons honey or maple syrup, to taste

Seasonings, add one:
2 sage leaves
2 juniper berries
1 teaspoon sumac
2 to 4 tablespoons chopped mint leaves to taste

Place the apples into a deep sauté pan or pot with the cider and set over medium-high heat. Cover and bring to a gentle boil and cook until the apples are very soft, about 20 minutes. Remove the lid and add salt, honey, and one of the seasonings and continue simmering until the sauce has thickened, another 10 minutes. Remove from the stove and taste. Adjust the seasonings.

CARAMELIZED SEED MIX

Sú Čhaŋháŋpšaša
Makes ½ cup

Caramelized Seed Mix

These seeds are so delicious you may find yourself eating the whole pan before they're served. Go ahead and double or triple the batch. They'll keep a long time in an airtight container. These are great on a salad or as a snack.

1 cup raw sunflower seeds, pepitas, and/or squash seeds
⅓ cup maple sugar

In a large, nonstick skillet, heat the seeds over medium-high heat until they begin to smell nutty, about 3 minutes. Stir in the maple sugar, stirring constantly until melted and the kernels are nicely coated. Transfer onto waxed paper or parchment to cool.

ROASTED IN THE SHELL SUNFLOWER SEEDS

Waȟčázi Tȟáŋka Sú Tȟákapi

Makes 1 cup

Make your own roasted sunflower seeds for a snack or to take to the ballpark for the next game.

1 cup raw sunflower seeds in the shell
2 tablespoons coarse salt
1 quart water

Preheat the oven to 400°F. Put the seeds, salt, and water into a saucepan and set over medium-high heat. Bring to a boil, reduce the heat, and simmer for about 15 to 20 minutes. Drain the water and spread the seeds out in a single layer on a baking sheet. Roast the seeds until crisp and flavorful, about 10 to 15 minutes. Cool and store in an airtight container.

INDIGENOUS GRANOLA

Sú Kpaŋkpáŋla
Makes about 4 to 5 cups

We keep this on hand for breakfasts and to garnish our sorbets. It also makes a delicious snack.

2 cups Toasted Sunflower Seeds, page 158
1 cup Toasted Pumpkin Seeds, page 158
½ cup popped amaranth grain, page 144
1 cup Corn Nuts, page 176
¼ cup hemp seeds
¼ cup maple syrup
3 tablespoons sunflower oil
Assorted dried cherries, blueberries, cranberries to taste

Preheat the oven to 300°F. Line a baking sheet with parchment paper. In a large mixing bowl, using your hands, mix together all of the ingredients except the dried fruit. (It's messy but fun if you get a kid to help.) Spread the mixture out on the parchment paper and bake until the ingredients are lightly toasted, about 10 minutes. Remove and cool before mixing in the dried fruit. Store in an airtight container.

Indigenous Granola

NATIVE GRANOLA BARS

Sú Kpaŋkpáŋla Obléthuŋ Kaȟyápi

Makes about 3 cups

A delicious snack, great topping for our sorbets, and delicious on salads and soups or baked squash, these bars are easy to make and will keep in a covered container for several weeks.

½ cup untoasted pumpkin seeds
½ cup untoasted sunflower seeds
1 tablespoon sunflower oil
¼ cup Puffed Wild Rice, page 175
¼ cup cracked Corn Nuts, page 176
1 cup dried cranberries
¼ cup dried blueberries
3 cups Sunny Butter, page 166

Preheat the oven to 325°F. Line a baking sheet with parchment paper or lightly grease it. In a small bowl, toss the pumpkin and sunflower seeds with just enough oil to lightly coat. Spread out on the baking sheet and toast until lightly browned and crisp, about 7 to 10 minutes. Remove and set aside.

A tablespoon at a time, add the wild rice to a dry skillet. Set over medium heat and puff the rice by shaking the pan until it pops. Remove and repeat with the rest of the wild rice. Set aside.

In a large bowl, mix together all of the ingredients and spread out onto the prepared baking sheet. Bake, rotating the pan every 7 to 10 minutes, until the surface is evenly dry and lightly browned, about 10 to 12 minutes.

When cool, cut into bars. Store in a covered container; best if kept refrigerated for up to 3 weeks.

Native Granola Bars

SEED SAVERS SNACKS

We roast the seeds of local vegetables—squash, pumpkins, sunflowers, maple seeds— to enjoy as snacks, work into sweets (cookies, granola, and granola bars), and garnish salads, soups, and stews. The process is easy, saves money, and makes excellent use of what too often is tossed into the compost pile. Once roasted, these may be kept in an airtight container and kept handy in the pantry. Season them with salt or dried herbs, or sweeten with maple sugar, and you are ready to go.

ROASTED MAPLE SEEDS
Čhaŋhásaŋ Sú Tȟákapi

It makes sense that the seeds of the trees that produce delicious sap would be sweet and edible, too. Maple seeds are best in the spring, when those whirligigs are fluttering in the wind.

Gather the green maple seeds, remove the outer casing, and scatter onto a baking sheet. Sprinkle with a little salt and maple sugar and bake at 350°F for about 5 to 8 minutes, shaking the pan occasionally.

TOASTED PUMPKIN AND SQUASH SEEDS
Wagmúsu ǧuǧú

Pumpkin and squash seeds are loaded with protein and fiber, and they make a terrific snack or crunchy addition to soups, stews, and salads. The process is easy.

Scoop out the seed mass of the squash or pumpkin; run under cold water. Soak the seeds for 2 to 4 hours in a bowl of cold, salted water (about half a teaspoon of coarse salt per cup of water). Rinse the seeds in a strainer and rub them between your fingers to loosen the pulp. Scatter the seeds on a towel to dry for several hours or overnight; they should be dry to the touch.

Toss the seeds with just enough sunflower or walnut oil to lightly coat. Spread the seeds out on a baking sheet and sprinkle with coarse salt. Roast in a preheated 350°F oven, shaking the pan occasionally until they are lightly browned and crisp, about 45 to 55 minutes. Cool on the pan and store in an airtight container.

TOASTED SUNFLOWER SEEDS
Waȟčázi sú

Toss raw sunflower seeds in a little sunflower oil to coat and spread out on a baking sheet. Roast in a preheated 350°F oven until they begin to brown and become crunchy, about 25 to 35 minutes. Remove and cool in an airtight container.

MAPLE BRULEED SQUASH WITH BLUEBERRIES

Wagmú Čhaŋháŋpi Akálapi nakúŋ Háza

Serves 4 to 6

We serve these tender, sweet squash treats on our cookie plate. They're delicious over sorbets and make a tasty snack.

1 pound winter squash, peeled, seeded, and cut into 2-inch chunks
1 tablespoon hazelnut oil
2 tablespoons maple syrup
Pinch salt
¼ cup toasted pepitas

Preheat the oven to 400°F. Toss the squash with the hazelnut oil and spread out onto a baking sheet so that none of the squash pieces are touching. Roast, turning frequently, until the squash is very tender and beginning to brown at the edges, about 30 minutes. Brush with the maple syrup and sprinkle with the salt and pepitas. Serve warm or at room temperature.

TOBACCO

Tobacco was cultivated by the older men in most tribes. Used primarily for ceremonies, it was also traded and used as currency. Tobacco is a unifying thread of communications between humans and spiritual powers. Dry tobacco was placed at the base of a tree or shrub from which medicine was gathered. To this day, a pinch is thrown into the water each day of wild rice gathering to assure calm weather and a bountiful harvest. When storms approached, families protected themselves by placing tobacco on a nearby rock, and it was placed at graves as an offering to the departed. Tobacco sealed peace treaties between tribes and individuals. To many tribes (e.g., the Ojibwe), tobacco continues to be a sacred plant.

PIPESTONE

Pipestone, in southwest Minnesota, not far from the South Dakota border, was a sacred center where the Lakota, Dakota, Yankton, and Sioux quarried rock for ceremonial pipes. The area was a neutral zone, where groups came in peace. No weapons were to be brought onto the sacred grounds. Dakota Sioux legend tells how Great Spirit sent a flood to cleanse the earth, and the red pipestone that remains is the blood of the ancestors. The stone belongs to all tribes and is used for nothing but to make pipes.

TEAS AND REFRESHING DRINKS

We enjoy a variety of teas brewed from local herbs and trees as a refreshment as well as drink them for their medicinal properties. In *Traditional Plant Foods of Canadian Indigenous Peoples,* Harriet V. Kuhnlein and Nancy J. Turner document how deeply our ancestors understood the curative properties of these plants. North American Native medicines share much with traditional Eastern medicines: all are grounded in a rich understanding of the natural world. When I began my journey, I could see that tribes on opposite ends of North America used the same plants for the same purposes, and then I realized my path and how much there is still to learn.

LABRADOR TEA
Ȟaȟáthuŋwaŋ Waȟpé

The Labrador plant, once steeped, makes a tea—sometimes called swamp tea—that is surprisingly close to English breakfast tea. The plants grow in thick, knee to waist-high banks in the wet, spongy, acidic soil of lowland bogs across North America. The evergreen foliage resembles that of a rhododendron—with leathery dark green to rusting to magenta leaves that roll under at the edges. Yellow fur covering the underside of the leaves gives off a powerful lemony aroma when crushed, making the plant easy to identify. The plant's fragrance and showy clusters of small white blossoms on the tips manifest from May through August.

CEDAR TEA
Ȟaŋté

Cedar is a sacred tree and, like sweetgrass and tobacco, is part of many ceremonies. It's used to purify homes, in sweat-lodge ceremonies, and as a medicine. The tea of simmered branches is used to treat fevers and rheumatic complaints, chest colds, and flu. This brew is delicious warm or cold and is simple to make. Just simmer 2 cups of fresh cedar in 4 cups of boiling water for about 10 minutes until the water becomes a golden color. Strain off the cedar and sweeten with maple syrup, to taste.

Cedar Tea

Labrador Tea

Chaga

MINT TEA
Čheyáka

Very refreshing, especially when served chilled, mint tea is delicious mixed with raspberry or blueberry juice. Simmer 4 cups of mint leaves in 2 cups of water.

BERGAMOT TEA
Waȟpé Waštémna

Bergamot has a minty flavor. It's a potent herb, so use a light touch. Simmer 4 cups of bergamot in 6 cups of water.

RASPBERRY LEAF TEA
Tȟakháŋheča Waȟpé

Raspberry leaf tea is delicious and restorative. It's a digestive, perfect served after a heavy meal. Simmer both the raspberry canes and the leaves in a pot covered with water for 20 minutes.

CHAGA
Tȟaŋpá Aíčhaǧe

Chaga is the mushroom that grows on the birch tree. It's loaded with antioxidants, and many claim that it fights cancer. It has a flavor reminiscent of a very mild coffee with chocolaty undernotes. To brew it, first dry the mushroom until hard, then grind it or smash it into chunks. Simmer in water for 20 minutes to 1 hour. It's delicious with any nut milk, especially hazelnut milk, and honey or maple syrup.

Chaga Sauce: Reduce the chaga tea until it's very dark and strong, and thin it with maple syrup or honey.

SUMAC LEMONADE
Čhaŋzí Sú Haŋpí

The staghorn sumac tree's fat clusters of berries ripen around mid-August into a burnished ruddy red. They make a pretty pink lemonade.

To make sumac lemonade, pick a dozen red clusters. Rub and crunch them and add to a gallon of cold water. Allow them to steep for 10 to 20 minutes. Strain the liquid through a fine-mesh strainer or a colander lined with cheesecloth into a pitcher. Sweeten to taste with honey or maple syrup.

THE FIREWATER MYTH

There is evidence to dispute the "drunken Indian" stereotype. Many tribes throughout the United States created spirits by fermenting corn mash, maple or birch sap, and fruit juices for use in social and religious gatherings prior to colonization. But once Europeans arrived, alcohol became a valued trade commodity exchanged for furs, land, and sexual favors.

The term "firewater" was used to describe the Native custom of testing the alcohol's strength (proof) by throwing it into a fire. If the alcohol was flammable, the Natives would consider it acceptable for purchase. Firewater was also a wicked brew of alcohol, tobacco juice, hot pepper, and/or opium. By the time Lewis and Clark traveled across the American West, most Indians they met were familiar with alcohol (Abbott, "American Indian and Alaska Native Aboriginal Use of Alcohol in the United States").

THE INDIGENOUS PANTRY

When I first started researching Native foods, I was fascinated with the idea of the food cache. I had read an old Lakota legend about a hermit who lived in woods far to the east who taught a brother and sister to bury their seeds and their harvest foods to keep them safe. Such legends, folktales, and stories provide insight to ancient cultures and are rich with meaning. When I discovered Buffalo Bird Woman's detailed account of an indigenous pantry, I was beyond excited. It was clear to me that all the dry foods, oils, salts, and seasonings kept buried or stored away for the long winters were the true base of the flavors of indigenous foods. Here was the best example of foods that people would be drawing on throughout the entire year. I can picture those ancestral pantries brimming with varieties of dried corn seeds and meals, dried squash rings, assorted vegetable flours, an apothecary of herbs and seasonings, ashes, salts, and roots.

As we design our restaurant, "The Sioux Chef—An Indigenous Kitchen," we are striving to recreate a modern indigenous kitchen fully stocked with preserved fruits, vegetables, fish, meats, and seasonings. We are constantly gathering and drying, grinding, and storing the natural and flavorful ingredients that surround us—bergamot, hyssop, tree seasonings, fruits, barks, seeds. Using modern appliances, we freeze freshly picked berries so we can enjoy them in their most simple form, without the excess salt and sugar inherent in pickling or canning.

Drying meats, fruits, and vegetables not only preserves them but concentrates and intensifies flavors for addition to soups, stews, and sauces. We also smoke and dry meats to enhance their flavors and add smoke and ash to other foods. Because nature does not create consistent products, we enhance the natural qualities of the foods we work with by choosing seasonings we have on hand.

Once the pantry is well stocked, improvising dishes and creating your own variations comes easily. Creating an indigenous kitchen for the modern world requires attention to the cycle of food and our responsibility to nurture ourselves, each other, and our mother earth.

SUNNY BUTTER

Waȟčázi Tȟáŋka Sú Iglí
Makes about 5 cups

We use this delicious spread in our cookies and granola, and as the base for several spreads. Store it in a covered container in the refrigerator for about a month.

4 cups unsalted toasted sunflower seeds
2 teaspoons smoked salt or coarse salt to taste
2 cups honey or maple syrup

Working in batches, put 1 cup of the sunflower seeds into a food processor fitted with a steel blade and grind. Add ½ teaspoon salt and ½ cup of the honey or maple syrup and process until a ball forms. Remove and repeat,

Chef's Note: Use these same proportions to make walnut, hazelnut, and other nut butters.

INDIGENOUS FLOURS

Aǧúyapi Blú Ikčéka

Just about any vegetable, fruit, seed, or grain can be ground into flour. Vegetables and fruits must be dehydrated first; seeds, grains, and nuts are toasted.

WILD RICE FLOUR

Psíŋ Blú

This flour is great for dusting fish before frying or to work into corn cakes. Whisk it into sauces and soups as a thickener. It will keep indefinitely in a covered container.

To make the flour, put the wild rice through a flour mill or grind in a food processor fitted with a steel blade. The more it is ground, the finer the flour.

VEGETABLE FLOUR

Watȟótȟó Blú

Squash, as well as many other dry-fleshed vegetables, makes excellent flour. These flours are loaded with vitamins and nutrients, are gluten free, and add robust flavor to soups, stews, sauces, and baked goods. It's not necessary to peel or seed the squash. The whole squash will dry and can be then ground into a lovely flour.

Many people are seeking alternatives to grain flours. Vegetable flours make delicious, nutritious alternatives to wheat and corn.

1. Slice the vegetable into ½ slices.
2. Arrange the slices on the racks of a food dehydrator or on racks set over a baking sheet and bake until thoroughly dry.
3. Put the vegetable through a flour mill or grind in a food processor. Store in an airtight container.

Chef's Note: Use this same method to make the following:

- Pumpkin flour
- Sunchoke flour
- Timpsula or turnip flour

Honey-Dried Squash Variation: Dip the sliced squash into a mix of 1 part honey to 2 parts water before setting on the drying rack.

Chef's Note: Reserve some of the dehydrated vegetables to use as garnishes for soups, stews, and salads.

Flours

ACORN MEAL FLOUR
Úta Blú

Acorns taste like a cross between hazelnuts and sunflower seeds. They are abundant, easy to store, high in protein, and very nutritious. They are nearly as important to Native Americans as corn, squash, and beans.

The Cherokee, Apache, Pima, Ojibwe, and most other Native American tribes across the oak-growing North and South America routinely harvested and used acorn nuts from oak trees.

Because acorns are very high in tannin, the dry-tasting substance associated with dry red wine, they need to be soaked before using. The flour will keep indefinitely in a covered container in a cool, dry place.

To start, gather the acorns and examine each one carefully. Discard any that are cracked, moldy, or wormy. Early in the season the shells are soft and easy to cut; later you may need a nutcracker to shell the acorn.

Put the acorns into a large pot and cover with water by 2 to 3 inches. Set over a high flame, bring to a boil, and cook until the water turns brown. Drain and repeat until the water is clear, about 3 to 5 times. Drain and pat dry.

Preheat the oven to 250°F. Arrange the acorns on a baking sheet in a single layer and bake until the nuts are firm, dry, and toasted, about 1½ to 2 hours. Remove from the oven and cool.

To make the flour, place the nuts into a food processor fitted with a steel blade and grind to the texture of cornmeal.

HAZELNUT FLOUR
Úma Blú

Hazelnuts are deliciously nutty, are a great source of oil, and make a wonderful flour. Place the shelled nuts in a single layer on a baking sheet and toast in a 350°F oven until they smell toasty, about 3 to 5 minutes. Wrap the nuts in a clean dishcloth and roll to remove the peels. Then grind them in a food processor fitted with a steel blade, a blender, a coffee grinder, or a spice mill. Store the flour in a covered container in the refrigerator or freeze.

CHESTNUT FLOUR
Úma Iyéčheča Blú

To make chestnut flour, chop peeled chestnuts, page 85, into small pieces. Dry in a food dehydrator or the oven at a low temperature until rock hard. Transfer to a flour mill, food processor, or coffee mill and grind to make a fine flour. Store in the freezer.

INDIGENOUS STOCKS

Waháŋpi Ikčéka kiŋ

Just about any indigenous ingredient used in a recipe can also become a stock, from wild rice to corn to mushrooms and root vegetables.

WILD RICE STOCK

Psíŋ Haŋpí

Do not discard wild rice cooking water. It makes an excellent cooking stock for soups, stews, and sauces. Wild rice stock is also the base for Wild Rice Sorbet, page 149.

CORN STOCK

Wagmíza Haŋpí

Save the corncobs after you've enjoyed boiled or roasted corn on the cob or you've cut the kernels for use in a recipe. Put the corncobs into a pot and cover with water by about 1 inch. Bring to a boil and partially cover. Reduce the heat and simmer until the stock tastes "corny," about 1 hour. Discard the cobs. Store the stock in a covered container in the refrigerator or freezer.

CEDAR BEAN STOCK

Ȟaŋté Apé úŋ Omníča Lolóbyapi Haŋpí

Reserve the leftover cooking liquid when preparing the Cedar-Braised Beans, page 36, for use in soups, stews, and sauces.

FISH, GAME, MEAT STOCK

Tȟaló Haŋpí

We make stock with just about everything in the larder, including vegetables (except greens) and bones (even smoked fish bones). Essential seasonings:

- Juniper
- Sage
- Cedar
- Mint

Juniper and cedar are aggressive flavors, so add seasoning with a light touch. You can always add more later on. Then add enough water to cover the ingredients completely and set over a low flame until the stock is flavorful. Cooking time will vary depending on the amount of liquid and the ingredients, but most stocks require cooking at least 2 to 3 hours.

Indigenous Stock can be made from many different ingredients

WOJAPE

Wóžapi
Makes about 4 to 6 cups

The scent of this traditional sauce simmering on the stove takes me back to my freewheeling six-year-old self. Our family relied on the local chokecherries I gathered as a kid. We'd spread a blanket under the trees and gather buckets full. There's no need to pit them because the pits drop to the bottom of the pot as the sauce becomes thick and lush. We'd sweeten it for a d essert or serve it as a tangy sauce for meat and game and vegetables, and as a dressing.

6 cups fresh berries—chokecherries or a mix of blueberries, raspberries,
  strawberries, elderberries, cranberries, blackberries
1 to 1½ cups water
Honey or maple syrup to taste

Put the berries and water into a saucepan and set over low heat. Bring to a simmer and cook, stirring occasionally, until the mixture is thick. Taste and season with honey or maple syrup as desired.

Wojape

SPROUTS

Čhamní

Makes 1 cup sprouts

Wild sprouts

Sunflower sprouts are the most delicious germinated seeds, more tender and sweeter than alfalfa, lentil, or radish. Unlike most of those sprouts, baby sunflowers germinate in soil. Here's how to sprout.

1. Drill drainage holes in the bottom of an old wood box and cover the drainage holes with pebbles. Add about 3 inches of soil to the box.
2. Soak 4 cups of unhulled sunflower seeds in a large bowl with plenty of water for 12 hours. Drain.
3. Scatter the seeds over the soil in one layer and press them onto the soil with your palm.
4. Sprinkle the seeds with water and cover with newspaper.
5. Sprinkle water over the newspaper once a day, until the sprouts begin to push the newspaper up, about 2 to 4 days. Remove the paper and continue watering the seeds daily, picking the seed hulls off the leaves after the small plants stand up.
6. When the first two leaves open, snip the sprouts with a scissors and enjoy.

PUFFED WILD RICE

Psíŋ Nabláȟyapi

Makes 2 cups

Like popcorn or puffed amaranth, puffed wild rice makes a terrific garnish for salads or soups and a great addition to griddled cakes and cookies. Light and crunchy, nutty tasting, it's a wonderful snack, too.

1 tablespoon sunflower oil
1 cup wild rice, rinsed
Pinch salt

Pat the rice with a clean cloth or paper towels so that it's thoroughly dry. Heat a heavy-bottomed saucepan over high heat. When the pot is hot, add the oil and wild rice. Cover the pan and shake vigorously to coat the wild rice thoroughly. Reduce the heat to medium and continue shaking until you can hear the rice popping. Sprinkle the rice with a little salt before serving.

RAMPS

You can almost smell ramps (wild leeks) before you find them in the woods. Buried in the damp leaves, they send up a subtle scent of crushed garlic and onions, announcing themselves. A member of the lily family, ramps are milder than garlic and not as harsh as onions. They resemble scallions with darker and broader green stalks and bright white bulbs. Unlike cultivated leeks, the entire plant is edible when seared, sautéed, or roasted. Use ramps as you would domesticated leeks, in soups, stews, omelets, and egg dishes.

CORN NUTS

Wagmíza Tȟákapi

Makes 2 to 2½ cups

Corn Nuts

We make these up in big batches to have on hand for snacks and to garnish salads and soups. Be careful! They're hard to stop eating.

2 cups Giant White Corn (also labeled as Maíz Mote Pelado)
4 tablespoons sunflower oil
1 tablespoon maple sugar
1 tablespoon sea salt
1 tablespoon sumac

Put the corn into a large bowl and add enough water to cover it by 2 inches. Soak 12 to 14 hours. Drain and rinse the corn and pat dry with a clean dish towel or paper towels.

Preheat the oven to 400°F. Line a baking sheet with parchment paper or lightly grease. Toss the corn with the oil and sprinkle with the maple sugar, salt, and sumac and spread out on the baking sheet in a single layer. Roast, stirring the kernels occasionally, until they are dark and crispy, about 25 to 35 minutes, watching that they don't burn. Remove and cool before storing in an airtight container.

DRIED MUSHROOMS

Dried Mushrooms

Dried wild mushrooms are one of our special kitchen ingredients. Once they are reconstituted, they are as delicious as fresh mushrooms and the soaking liquid adds terrific flavor to sauces, soups, stews, and stocks.

Generally, 1 cup of fresh mushrooms will yield about ½ cup of dried mushrooms. To dry wild mushrooms, use a dehydrator or arrange them on a screen and set in a cool, dry area for several days. Store in an airtight container.

Packaged dried wild mushrooms are available in the produce aisle of co-ops and supermarkets.

DRIED APPLE SLICES

Rings of dried apples make pretty garnishes to soups, stews, and salads and are a nice snack. Simply core the apples and remove the seeds, then slice horizontally, about ¼ inch thick. Use a dehydrator or arrange the slices on a screen and place in the oven set on a very low heat until the slices are leathery to the touch. Store in an airtight container.

Packaged dried apple rings are available in the produce aisle of co-ops and supermarkets.

TAPPING TREES—
MORE THAN MAPLE

Most people associate syrup with maple trees. Although maple trees do yield the highest volume and concentration of sap, with the highest sugar content, there are plenty of other trees that share their sweet gifts with us.

BOXELDER (AKA MANITOBA MAPLE)

This tree gives only about half the syrup of maples, but it is tasty.

BUTTERNUT

This tree will not give quite as much sap as
a maple tree, but it is worth tapping.

BIRCH

This tree produces sap with a lower sugar content with a
slightly tannic edge that works nicely in savory dishes.

SYCAMORE

This tree produces a sap that's a bit lower in sugar content
than maple sap and has lovely butterscotch overtones.

DOUGLAS FIR SUGAR

Sometimes called Wild Sugar, this sugar was once gathered from the
branches of individual Douglas fir trees and used as a sweetener. It's
not easy to find. The sugar is produced from the branch tips of trees having
abundant exposure to the sun and good soil moisture during the hottest
days of midsummer. It appears as white, frost-like globules on the
branches and can be gathered into a container and used as a sweetener.

John Nickaboine boiling maple sap, circa 1930

MAPLE WINE AND VINEGAR

Wherever maple trees were tapped, maple wine and vinegar must have been made.
Toward the end of the sugar-making season in the month of April, the sap loses
much of its sweetness and when boiled down will not make sugar but will ferment
into wine and then vinegar. It's made by allowing the sap to ferment in a jug set in
a dark corner for a few weeks.

NATIVE HERBS AND SEASONINGS

Wíčahiyutapi Ikčéka

BERGAMOT

The pretty, narrow, tubular flowers are maroon, magenta, and lilac and resemble a chrysanthemum atop a two-foot-high erect stalk. This member of the mint family attracts hummingbirds and helps repel mosquitoes and gnats. It's wonderful in apple jelly and wine.

Bergamot

SAGE

Dusty green leaves infuse meats and soups with an earthy, piney flavor.

CEDAR

Great for braising meats and simmering into grains and stews.

Cedar

MINT

Bright mint works best fresh. It tends to lose its punch in heat.

JUNIPER

Those tiny dusty blue berries are peppery and give foods a ginny edge.

STAGHORN SUMAC

This northern sumac grows along ditches and on the borders of forests. Its deep red berries have a citrusy tang.

Juniper

MUSTARD

Mustard grows wild and makes a very peppery green in a salad or as a garnish. Collect the seeds and you have a wonderful spice.

ROSE HIPS

Dried or fresh, rose hips add a light citrusy note to stocks and soups.

Staghorn Sumac

CULINARY ASH
Čhaȟóta

Culinary ash seasoning dates back thousands of years. Just as smoke was an important, primal flavor that cues our original use of fire to transform raw ingredients into delicious foods, burning trees and the hard, inedible parts of plants is an ancient method of creating flavorful spices.

The tastes of ash seasoning vary depending on the plant used—corncobs, sage leaves, juniper berries, rose hips, sumac—and the ash adds color and interest to many dishes. To create ash, hold the food over a flame with tongs or set it on a grill or under a broiler, rotating it until it's thoroughly blackened. Remove and place on a baking sheet until it is cool enough to handle.

Any food can be "ashed," but here are those we like using the best:

- **Corn ash** is slightly sweet, dark, and a bit creamy.
- **Sage ash** is peppery and assertive.
- **Juniper ash** will turn the foods it seasons a dark, inky blue and add an earthy, piney, peppery note.

STAGHORN SUMAC

Pulling sumac berries for seasoning

Staghorn sumac grows throughout the upper Midwest and Northeast, winged sumac in the East and South, and smooth sumac throughout the east and central United States and the West. There are nonpoisonous sumacs that grow in open and edge habitats. The biggest difference between these varieties of sumac and poisonous sumac is the color of the berries. Poison sumac berries are white; all others are red or ruddy.

To use sumac as a seasoning, harvest the clusters and pull the berries from the branches. Spread out on a piece of parchment to dry for about a day. Then place the dried berries in a bag and crush. Store in an airtight container out of direct sunlight.

Making ash

MINERAL SALT

Many years ago, Native people gathered salt by following the animals to the salt licks. Salt from the oceans was traded and used as currency.

Seasoned salts are easy to make and handy to have on hand. To make an herbed salt, rinse and dry the herb well. Allow it to air-dry for a few days. Then immerse it in a jar of coarse salt. The salt will draw moisture from the herb and further dry it while the herb will infuse the salt with flavor. You can make these seasoned salts with just one herb or with a mix of the following herbs: sage, cedar, juniper, mint.

SMOKED SALT

Smoked salts are available in the spice aisles of supermarkets, in specialty shops, and online. Making your own is relatively easy:

2 cups wood chips soaked in cold water for 1 hour, drained
2 cups coarse salt

Prepare the grill for indirect heat (putting the hot coals on one side so that there is a cool side to work from). Toss the drained wood chips on the coals. Spread the salt in a thin layer in an aluminum foil pan and place it on the grate away from the fire. Cover the grill and adjust the vent holes for medium heat. Smoke the salt for 1 hour. Remove, allow to cool at room temperature, and then store in a covered jar.

INDIGENOUS PARTNERS
AND GUIDES

When I began my work on indigenous foods, I was surprised to find so little published information on the subject. The cookbooks featured recipes for Native American–European fusion—such as buffalo meatloaf with ketchup or stews using Campbell's Cream of Mushroom Soup. I dug into history books and academic texts, and interviewed elders to help me piece together bits of information. Little did I know that other like-minded Native chefs and educators were on a similar journey.

In 2013, Chef Nephi Craig of the White Mountain Apache invited me to his Native American Culinary Association's (NACA) "Native Chef's Symposium" at the Sonoran Desert Museum outside Tucson, Arizona. The Native chefs I met shared their unique perspective on the foods of their regions. Over the years, the passion and knowledge of these colleagues have inspired and energized me. Thanks to their support, I've devoted my life to researching, understanding, and developing Native foods for the future.

Here are stories and recipes from these chefs, educators, and advocates who are shaping a new indigenous cuisine. These dishes are as varied and spirited as are their creators, and they reflect the shared values of, and respect for, our ancestral foods.

CHEF RICH FRANCIS

Owner and Chef, the Seventh Fire Hospitality Group

....

SCALLOPS WITH THREE SISTERS REDUCTION AND FOUR MEDICINES

Serves 4

As a finalist in Canada's Top Chef, Rich Francis has brought the indigenous foods of his home—Six Nations, Ontario—to a wider audience. His dishes are innovative, inspiring, and beautiful, and they present Native cuisine, rooted in tradition, in a contemporary light. This appetizer is a staple on his menus.

In the original recipe, the scallops are served in a smudge bowl (abalone shell) and garnished drizzled with a three sisters reduction (a sauce of corn, beans, and squash), scented with vanilla and topped with a generous amount of sturgeon caviar. We have taken a few liberties by using local flavors. The Four Medicines—tobacco, sweetgrass, sage, and cedar—smoking under the bowl add their scents and enhance the experience. "This is my baby," Francis says. "I've seen it grow into what it is now, perfect in its simplicity. Everything I do as a chef is to contribute to or benefit First Nation Cuisine as a whole. It's a really exciting time for our food that belongs up there with the other global cuisines."

6 to 8 ounces sea scallops

Smoked salt, page 183

2 tablespoons sunflower oil

¼ cup chopped wild onion or ramps

1 ear corn, kernels cut from the cob
   and reserved

1 cup cooked white beans

1 cup cubed Griddled Maple Squash, page 33

2 tablespoons maple vinegar

Maple syrup to taste

Water or corn stock, page 170, as needed

1 tablespoon finely chopped cedar

Generous pinch sage ash, page 182

Pat the scallops dry and season with the smoked salt. In a large ovenproof skillet, heat the oil over medium-high until almost smoking. Add the scallops and cook on both sides until nicely browned and firm to the touch, about 2 to 4 minutes per side.

Put the onions, corn, beans, and squash into a small saucepan and add the maple vinegar and maple syrup. Set over medium-high heat and bring to a simmer. Turn into a food processor fitted with a steel blade or into a blender and add a little water or corn stock to thin as necessary. Season with more of the smoked salt. Spoon the platter or individual plates. Serve the scallops on top of the salsa sprinkled with the cedar and sage ash.

The four medicines—tobacco, sweetgrass, sage, and cedar—may be lit under the serving dish or individual bowls.

CHEF KARLOS BACA

NAVAJO TEA–SMOKED QUAIL WITH MANOOMIN FRITTER, PICKLED CHOLLA, AND LICHII SAUCE

Serves 2 to 4

Karlos Baca, trained in classic French cuisine, brings his talent and skill to foods of his home in the Four Corners region of Colorado. Yucca root, pine needles, Navajo tea—the foods he forages speak of the landscape and Native histories. "I'd probably seen them a million times hiking, but I didn't know you could eat them," he said. "I want people to know that this food is a valuable part of our culture."

As founder of The Taste of Native Cuisine, Chef Baca brings together Native American chefs and cooks to provide the traditional wild-harvested and hunted foods to tribes in the Four Corners region. He works with youth, and in Native communities, and tends his own heritage garden.

4 quail

FOR THE SMOKE

3 small bundles Navajo tea, broken and soaked for 5 minutes

6 wild onions, roughly chopped

1 tablespoon three-leaf sumac

Place mixture in smoker tray and smoke quail at 250°F for 1 hour. If you would like a crispier skin, pan-fry in duck fat until golden.

FOR THE FRITTERS

1½ cups cooked wild rice, page 81

¼ cup thinly sliced wild onion or ramps

1 duck egg

¼ cup wild rice flour, page 167
   (mesquite flour is also a tasty alternative)

1 tablespoon duck fat

Salt and pepper to taste

Mix all ingredients and form into 2-inch patties. Fry until golden brown.

FOR PICKLED CHOLLA

½ cup cooked cholla buds

¼ teaspoon three-leaf sumac

¼ teaspoon chiltipin chiles

1 bay leaf

2 cups water

¼ cup apple cider vinegar

¼ cup salt

In a saucepan, bring all ingredients to a boil and let simmer 10 minutes. Remove from heat and refrigerate overnight. Store in brine for up to a month.

FOR LICHII SAUCE

1 cup red chile sauce (I prefer smoked ancho for this recipe,
    but a New Mexico red chile works great also)

2 tomatoes

¼ of an onion

1 red pepper

¼ teaspoon minced garlic

3 tablespoons honey (maple syrup can also be used)

2 tablespoon butter

1 tablespoon salt

Flame-char tomato, onion, and pepper until blackened. Sweat garlic in duck fat. Add chile sauce, tomato, onion, pepper, and honey and simmer 10 minutes. Blend and add butter.

NOURISHING TRADITION

Good food is created from experience and with care, honed with technique and skill, and enriched with memory. It has value well beyond money, though some people may try to monetize the work of others for their own personal gain. In the hands of people who have the patience to learn and master their craft, and the love and drive to share it with others, all that we hold sacred will survive.

CHEF LOIS ELLEN FRANK

CORIANDER-CURED ELK WITH DRIED CHOKECHERRY SAUCE

Serves 6

Lois Ellen Frank, James Beard Award–winning author of *Foods of the Southwest Indian Nations,* inspires us all. Based in Santa Fe, New Mexico, she is a Native foods historian and photographer devoted to documenting foods and lifeways of our Southwest tribes. A PhD in anthropology, she applies academic rigor to her own story with heart, soul, and skill. Working with Walter Whitewater, a self-taught Navajo chef, she's created Red Mesa Cuisine, a unique catering company that specializes in indigenous locally sourced sustainable foods.

"Native American Cuisine is so alive right now thanks to the many people preparing foods of their ancestors using ingredients from their past," she writes. "The movement today—the Indigenous Food Movement—is keeping our Traditional Ecological Knowledge or TEK alive for generations to come. Food is our medicine and it nourishes not only our bodies but our spirits, and our minds. It keeps alive the knowledge of who we are and where we came from. Food is part of our identity." Elk tenderloin may be unfamiliar to many, but it's worth seeking out. The meat is tender and delicious, richer tasting than venison. But if it's unavailable, venison works nicely, too.

CORIANDER RUB

2 teaspoons whole coriander

1 teaspoon whole cumin seed

1 teaspoon fennel seed

1 teaspoon whole black pepper

1 teaspoon dried thyme

1 teaspoon dried New Mexico or Anaheim red chile powder

1 teaspoon salt

1 elk tenderloin (approximately 2 pounds)

1 tablespoon olive oil

DRIED CHOKECHERRY SAUCE

½ cup dried or fresh chokecherries

3 cups black cherry juice

2 cups water

¾ cups dried tart and sweet Bing black cherries (pits removed)

Prepare the meat by trimming any fat from the elk tenderloin if there is any. Set aside.

Combine the dry ingredients. Place the dry ingredient mixture in a small baking pan and toast them in a dry skillet or in the oven for approximately 5 minutes, or until they are golden brown. Be careful not to burn the spices, as this will affect the flavor of the rub. You want to bring out the flavor of each spice by toasting it but you do not want to burn any of them. Remove from the skillet or oven and let cool. In a spice grinder, grind together the spices.

Remove from the grinder and rub the spice mixture onto both sides of the elk tenderloin to cover all of the meat. Place the elk tenderloin in a baking pan, cover with plastic wrap and let sit overnight in the refrigerator.

To make the sauce, combine the chokecherries with the black cherry juice in a medium-sized saucepan. Cook over medium heat for approximately 15 minutes, stirring occasionally until it is thicker. Add the water, bring to a boil, then reduce heat and simmer for another 20 minutes, uncovered, until the sauce has reduced by about half. Remove from the heat and pass the sauce through a fine mesh strainer. Return it to the saucepan.

Add the dried cherries to the strained sauce and cook for another 10 minutes until the dried cherries are soft. If your sauce is not thick enough, you can remove half of it, place the sauce in a blender and blend until smooth. Return the sauce to the saucepan with the unblended sauce in it and stir together.

The next day, remove the elk tenderloin from the refrigerator. Preheat the oven to 400°F. In a medium-sized skillet, over high heat, heat the olive oil until hot but not smoking. Sear the elk tenderloin for approximately 3 minutes on all of the sides then remove from the heat until it is completely seared on all sides. Place the elk tenderloin in a roasting pan and the bake for approximately 8 to 12 minutes for medium rare and longer for more well done meat. Remove from the oven and let rest for several minutes. Slice the tenderloin and serve hot with some of the dried black cherry sauce spooned on top.

CHEF ANDREA MURDOCH

INCA TRAIL MIX
Makes about 6½ cups

Chef Andrea Murdoch, in a quest to understand her Inca ancestry, has been researching and working with a variety of foods that are as ancient as they are nutritious. "Take quinoa, a staple of my ancestors, with a long and important history," she says. "Quinoa is small, lightweight, and high in protein, so it was carried by soldiers when they went on patrol or hunted. It is such an important plant, it warrants an animal sacrifice in offering for a good crop. Today, it's of special interest to those following gluten-free or vegan diets. I created this trail mix snack for the participants in a walk/run event to spread awareness of PTSD suffered by so many of those who have served our country on the battlefield."

This easy-to-make, delicious snack keeps nicely in a covered container for several months. Scatter it over salads or vegetable dishes, or use it to garnish soups.

1¾ cups quinoa
1¾ cups amaranth
1¼ cups squash seeds
2 tablespoons sunflower oil
2 cups dried blueberries
⅓ cup plus 2 tablespoons agave nectar or maple syrup

Preheat the oven to 350°F. In a fine-mesh strainer, rinse the quinoa under cool water and let it drain. Spread it out evenly on a baking sheet and dry in the oven for about 10 minutes, stirring midway through. For a toasty flavor, continue cooking an additional 5 minutes. Transfer to a large mixing bowl.

Set a 4-inch-deep pan over high heat and add a few tablespoons of amaranth to pop the grain. It will jump like popcorn. Pop the amaranth in batches and add it to the mixing bowl.

Toss the fresh squash seeds in sunflower oil and spread on a baking sheet. Roast in the preheated oven until the seeds are amber in color, about 10 minutes. Add to the mixing bowl.

Add the blueberries to the mixing bowl along with the agave and stir to combine. Spread the mix out evenly onto two baking sheets and return to the oven for 6 minutes. Stir and continue baking for an additional 6 minutes. Remove and cool thoroughly. Store in an airtight container for about a week or freeze.

CHEF BRIAN TATSUKAWA

J. D. KINLACHEENY'S CHILCHIN (SUMAC) PUDDING
Serves 4 to 6

Chef Brian Tatsukawa is chef instructor and department chair at Navajo Technical University, Crownpoint, New Mexico. He teaches and inspires young Native chefs by providing them opportunities to explore their heritage and culture through the dishes they create. We first met at the Native Chef Symposium organized by Chef Nephi Craig. The following student recipes reflect Chef Brian's guidance and wisdom.

At an event in Idyllwild, California, on top of the San Jacinto Mountains, Chef Terri Ami, one of Chef Brian's students, and I were pitted against Chef Freddie Bitsoie and Chef Felicia Cocotzin Ruiz in a lighthearted cooking competition judged by Chef Loretta Barrett Oden, radio personality Evan Kleinman, and our dear friend Shane Plumer. Chef Teri and I took first place and were given a special handmade pot as an award. These young, talented chefs are the future of indigenous food.

1½ **quarts water**
½ **cup dry apricots**
4 **tablespoons dried ground sumac berries**
1 **cup dry-roasted white ground corn**
½ **cup honey**
2 **tablespoons roasted pine nuts**

In a medium-sized bowl, add 2 cups water and the dried apricots to rehydrate until soft. Strain the apricots and save the juice. Set aside the rehydrated apricots.

In a medium saucepan, add the remaining water, ground sumac, and dry corn. Bring to a boil and stir continuously. After the mixture has thickened into a pudding consistency, add ¼ cup honey and stir together.

In a small sauté pan, roast the pine nuts over medium heat until golden brown, about 2 to 4 minutes.

In a small saucepan, add the apricot juice and ¼ cup honey. Bring to a boil and stir until thickened into a syrup.

To serve, put ½ cup of the sumac pudding into a bowl. Top with 2 to 4 rehydrated apricots, ½ teaspoon of the apricot syrup, and sprinkle with pine nuts.

TERRI AMI'S BLUE CORN MUSH

Serves 4 to 6

1½ cups water
½ teaspoon cedar ash, sifted
½ cup cold water
1 cup blue cornmeal

Optional
¼ cup local honey or agave or your choice of sweetener
1 cup local berries

Bring the water to a boil in a medium saucepan. Add the sifted cedar ash to the boiling water and stir until combined. Reduce the heat to medium-high.

In a small bowl, stir together the cold water and the blue cornmeal. Whisk the cornmeal mixture into the hot water, continuing to whisk until the cornmeal is cooked through and the consistency is close to that of cream of wheat or thicker. Sweeten to taste and serve, warm or cold, with fresh berries if desired.

CHEF FREDDIE BITSOIE

CORN BROTH
Makes about 2 quarts

Freddie Bitsoie, executive chef at the renowned Mitsitam Café at the National Museum of the American Indian in Washington, D.C., is one of the most sought-after educators and presenters. With a deep knowledge of art history and anthropology, Freddie shares his passion for Navajo (Diné) foods with wit and panache. His simple, elegant recipes are as inspiring as they are accessible.

"This broth is a workhorse in our kitchen; easy to make and more delicious as it simmers on the back of the stove," he says. To make a hearty soup or stew, add smoked fish or duck. Add soaked hominy or beans for a nutritious meal. It will keep several days in the refrigerator and freezes beautifully.

6 ears fresh corn, shucked
½ cup fresh or frozen corn kernels
3 stalks celery, roughly chopped
3 carrots, roughly chopped
3 cloves garlic, minced
4 sprigs fresh thyme
2 bay leaves
Salt and pepper to taste
4 quarts of water

Combine all of the ingredients, except for the salt and pepper, in a pot. Bring to a boil, then turn the heat down to a simmer. Simmer for about 3 hours. Strain the broth and discard the vegetables. Using a paper towel, strain the broth again for clarity. Pour the broth back into the pot. Place over medium heat and reduce it by three-fourths. Season with salt and pepper, to taste. Check the seasoning before serving. Serve warm or hot.

FELICIA COCOTZIN RUIZ

TWO-FRUIT JAM SCATTERED WITH SEEDS

Makes about 1 pint

Chef Felicia is an inspiration. Her Facebook and Instagram posts showcase her thoughtful, authentic plant-based recipes, all rooted in the history and culture of the Southwest. They reflect the bold flavors of this deeply spiritual place.

This jam is great on mesquite crackers, on blue corn pancakes, or in amaranth porridge.

1 pound tomatillos, husked, washed, and chopped
1 pound xoconostle,* cut in half, seeds removed with a spoon, peeled
¾ to 1 cup honey
1 cup water
½ teaspoon sea salt

Put all of the ingredients in a large saucepan and bring to a boil. Reduce the heat to simmer, stir well, and cook for about 45 minutes, until mixture has the consistency of jam. The jam will thicken even more once cooled and will keep for about 6 months refrigerated in a tightly covered container.

*Xoconostle is the fruit of the nopal cactus.

VALERIE SEGREST

WILD BERRIES WITH AMARANTH
Serves 2

A native nutrition educator who focuses on local, traditional foods, Valerie Segrest is a member of the Muckleshoot tribe. She serves her community as the coordinator of the Muckleshoot Food Sovereignty Project and as the Traditional Foods and Medicines Program Manager. She is coauthor with Elise Krohn of *Feeding the People, Feeding the Spirit: Revitalizing Northwest Coastal Indian Food Culture.*

Huckleberries grow throughout the Pacific Northwest. "Some are bright red with a bitter punch; others are as big as grapes and royal purple," Valerie and her coauthor write. "Ceremonies, spiritual journeys, harvesting and honor songs, careful ecological managements all celebrate the huckleberries' noble role in our culture."

This dish makes a delicious breakfast. It's good with any wild berries you might wish to use.

1 cup amaranth
Water
Pinch salt
1 cup huckleberries or any wild berries
1 tablespoon maple syrup
2 teaspoons balsamic vinegar

Put the amaranth in a bowl, add enough water to cover by 1 inch, and set aside to soak overnight. Drain in a colander and rinse under cold running water. Add the amaranth to a pot with enough water to cover and add a pinch of salt. Bring to a boil and then reduce the heat to a simmer. Cover and cook for about 8 to 10 minutes; drain off any unabsorbed water.

Put the berries, just enough water to cover the bottom of the pot, syrup, and vinegar into a small saucepan. Set over low heat and gently simmer until the berries soften and begin to burst, about 2 to 5 minutes. Spoon the berries over the amaranth and serve warm or at room temperature.

FEASTS OF THE MOON

Each tribe looks to the seasons to mark time guided by the moon and stars, weather and light. There's no Gregorian calendar to dictate the holidays. Rather, each tribe's intimate relationship with the earth is marked by thirteen full moons throughout the year with traditions uniquely anchored in time and place. Take the many different names for a September moon: Assiniboin, "The Moon of the Yellow Leaf"; Cherokee, "The Moon of the Nut Harvest"; Shawnee, "The Moon of the Pawpaw"; Ojibwe, "Leaves Changing Color Moon."

The Sioux Chef honors full moons with special pop-up dinners that feature traditional music, drumming, spoken word poetry, and prayer. These efforts help build community. We've selected several menus from these various feasts to illustrate how our meals are presented. We hope they'll help you as you plan your own celebrations.

SPIRIT PLATE
WANÁǦI WAÉKIČIHNAKAPI

Respect for Mother Earth and gratitude for her unrequited gifts are central to our traditional feasts.

Before we begin, we offer a Spirit Plate filled with samples of the food we will be sharing and we set it out in memory of those who cannot be physically present but who join us spiritually.

They may be deceased, incarcerated, ill, unable to travel, or not yet born. The food on this plate feeds the mysteries of life. It is an offering of thanks for all that we have received from the plants and animals who nourish us and have given their lives so that we may continue ours.

We pray for their continued abundance and protection. We pray that all nations will have food and water.

DINNER OF THE FLOWER MOON
WAABIGWANII-GIIZIS

To honor spring, the season that breaks through the iron clasp of monotonous winter, this menu showcases the first fresh foods to appear: sorrel, ramps, and maple (a sweet reward). Right before this dinner, held in Northfield, Minnesota, our staff headed into the woods to pick spruce tips, connecting us all to the powerful energy of spring.

OLD-FASHIONED RABBIT STEW, PAGE 112
AMARANTH CRACKERS, PAGE 60
SPRUCE TIPS

DRIED RABBIT, PAGE 115
SMOKED FOREST MUSHROOM
GRIDDLED MAPLE SUNCHOKE OR SQUASH, PAGE 33
SORREL
DRIED CHAGA

SWEET PEA PUREE
SMOKED TROUT, PAGE 89
BALSAM FIR PUREE, PUFFED WILD RICE, PAGE 175

ACORN AND WILD RICE CAKES, PAGE 143
DRIED APPLE SLICES, PAGE 177
SUNFLOWER COOKIES, PAGE 135

DINNER OF THE CHOKECHERRY MOON
CANPASAPA WI

July brings chokecherries, an iconic and important food throughout the Great Plains region. It is the basis of our foundational sauce, Wojape, the primary ingredient in many of our sauces, soups, salad dressings, and sweets. What better way to recognize the chokecherry's significant role in our culture than to create an Indigenous Foods Retreat at the Coteau des Prairies Lodge in North Dakota on the tip of the Sisseton–Wahpeton Sioux Reservation. We gathered people from all walks of life who wanted to learn about, forage, and cook chokecherries, gooseberries, buffalo berries, and all the wild foods on this wide-open, plentiful land. Under the blessing of the full chokecherry moon, we shared stories, legends, and knowledge of indigenous ways.

RABBIT STEW, PAGE 112
TIMPSULA CAKES, PAGE 86
WOJAPE, PAGE 173

CEDAR-BRAISED BISON, PAGE 120
CORN CAKES, PAGE 51
ELDERBERRY
WILD RICE PILAF PAGE 84

BISON WASNA, PAGE 125
PUFFED WILD RICE, PAGE 175
AMARANTH CRACKERS, PAGE 60

SWEET CORN SORBET, PAGE 147
SUNFLOWER COOKIES, PAGE 135
RASPBERRY–ROSE-HIP SAUCE, PAGE 142

DINNER OF THE MIDSUMMER MOON
MONINGWUNKAUNIG AND
AABITA-NIIBINO-GIIZIS

Honor the Earth, founded by Winona LaDuke, works to protect indigenous lands threatened by the exploration, drilling, and transport of oil, especially via pipelines. This dinner, held in Nisswa, Minnesota, reflects the flavors of our clear cold lakes and deep woods and Ojibwe traditions. Wild rice, fish, game, and corn from the region embody a message of bounty. In sharing this meal, we recommitted to each other and to caring for our valuable resources. The environmental issues faced by indigenous people are more urgent today than ever.

BRAISED SUNCHOKES, PAGE 32
WILD GREENS, PAGE 25

SMOKED DUCK, PAGE 106
SMOKED WHITEFISH, PAGE 89

GRILLED CORN WITH WILD GREENS PESTO, PAGE 24

MAPLE–SAGE ROASTED VEGETABLES, PAGE 46

WILD GREEN AND BERRY SALAD WITH
POPPED AMARANTH, PAGE 144

PUMPKIN SEEDS AND CORN COOKIES, PAGE 138

SUNFLOWER COOKIES, PAGE 135

FEAST OF THE WILD RICE MOON
MAOOMINIKE-GIIZIS

In the late summer, all across the Great Lakes region, families set up rice camps and spend several weeks harvesting wild rice. When the rice has been threshed and winnowed, and is ready to store throughout the year, they gather to feast. This dinner, hosted with Wozupi Tribal Gardens of the Mdewakanton Sioux, celebrates the fall harvest and the bounty that comes from this tribal farm. The dishes rely on the preservation methods for storing food through the winter. Although we no longer need to preserve food to survive, we do appreciate the bold flavors that preservation adds to a dish.

WILD RICE–CRUSTED WALLEYE, PAGE 90

MAPLE–SAGE ROASTED VEGETABLES, PAGE 46

CRISPY BEAN CAKES, PAGE 38
WOJAPE, PAGE 173

GRILLED CORN WITH WILD GREENS PESTO, PAGE 24

BLUEBERRY SORBET AND PUFFED WILD RICE, PAGE 175

DINNER OF THE GREAT SPIRIT MOON
GICHI-MANIDOO-GIIZIS

The elders of Nett Lake, Minnesota, have stories to tell, and when we go there to cook in the late fall, we are eager to listen. They share memories of running through the forests following secret paths to the most prized wild foods. The ancestral power of these tales never fails to hit us full force. We learn of those times before diabetes devastated the tribe's health, of how fear and mistrust became the cultural norm. In our work showing how easy it is to forage and prepare these healthy indigenous foods, we are connecting the residents to their past and their future, restoring our vibrant culture and our pride.

WHITE BEAN AND WINTER SQUASH SOUP, PAGE 70

SMOKED DUCK, PAGE 106
SWEET POTATO

WILD RICE PILAF, PAGE 84

CEDAR-BRAISED BISON, PAGE 120,
AND HOMINY, PAGE 31

GRIDDLED MAPLE SQUASH, PAGE 33

FEAST OF THE SORCERER AND THE EAGLE
MIXTECO-INSPIRED MENU

Indigenous cuisines throughout the Americas are extremely diverse, as showcased in this menu we created with Oaxacan chef Neftali Durán. He and his team traveled to St. Paul, Minnesota, for a celebration of indigenous Mixteco flavors featuring precolonial foods. As Chef Neftali offered prayers with the Spirit Plate, we honored our shared history, our struggles, and our strength.

TIAKUI YA'A (FISH CURED IN LIME)

AGUACHILE DE HUACHINANGO
CHILI OIL
TOSTADO AMARANTO
SPICY SHRIMP AND AVOCADO SALSA WITH CORN CRISPS

NDKU U VIDIA (HOMINY SOUP)

NAÑA ÑA NA MOLE
(SMOKED DUCK TAMALE, PAGE 57)

IXTAÁ NDUNCHI (BRAISED HEIRLOOM
BLACK BEANS, PAGE 36)
FRESH TORTILLAS

BLACK BEAN
COMAL-TOASTED TORTILLA
PRESERVED HIBISCUS
SALSA VERDE
EPAZOTE

NIEVE ÑA TICHÍ (AVOCADO SORBET
AND CHOCOLATE MOLE)

OWAMNI AND THE BUFFALO SKY

Owamni is the Dakota name for the great waterfalls now known as the St. Anthony Main Mississippi River Waterfront, a spiritual landmark for the Dakota. Buffalo Sky is the legend of a hunter who searched for the reason the buffalo went missing. He followed their tracks to the far north that led up a mountain and then disappeared into the night sky where they now shine as Northern Lights. They are waiting for the right time to return and live as one with us again. This, our first pop-up dinner, was held near the historic St. Anthony Falls.

DRIED RABBIT, PAGE 115
HOMINY CAKES, PAGE 53
TOASTED WALNUT
RASPBERRY–ROSE-HIP SAUCE, PAGE 142
DANDELION

CEDAR-BRAISED BEANS, PAGE 36
SMOKED WHITEFISH, PAGE 89

BISON RIBS, PAGE 118
PUFFED WILD RICE, PAGE 175
MASHED SWEET POTATO
WATERCRESS

SMOKED DUCK, PAGE 106
DRIED BLUEBERRY
AMARANTH CRACKERS, PAGE 60
TOASTED PEPITAS

MAPLE SQUASH SORBET, PAGE 149
CARAMELIZED SEED MIX, PAGE 152

ACKNOWLEDGMENTS

New Native American Cuisine is an emerging trend, but it is not solitary work. It is collaboration. We have to do this together. We call it "indigenous partnerships" — all ethnic groups working together where the indigenous agenda is the priority.

— Lois Ellen Frank

This book comes into the world thanks to the commitment, skill, passion, and knowledge of many amazing people who continue to bless and enrich my life. The Sioux Chef Team, each of you is invaluable: Brian Yazzie, Tashia Hart, Mike and Darius Willard, Andrea Weber, Nancy Sartor, Vern Defoe, Jenean Gilmore, and Christine Werner, who began this journey with us. Those who share indigenous knowledge: Diane Wilson (Dream of Wild Health), Rebecca Yoshino (Wozupi Tribal Gardens), Winona LaDuke, Elizabeth Hoover, Rowen White, Loretta Barret Oden, Simone Senogles, Nathan Ratner, Tejal Rao, Jed Portman, John T. Edge, John Currence, Christopher Kornmann, Seed Savers Exchange, Mashkiki Gardens, Little Earth of United Tribes, and Coteau des Prairies Lodge. Jody Eddy, for connecting us to so many resources; Chef Lenny Russo, mentor and friend; Ben Gessner of the Minnesota Historical Society; Dawi Dakhóta Iápi Okhódakičhiye for his translations.

Our family includes not just those we are directly related to but the incredible people who have supported us through the years: my mother, Joann Conroy; and my sister, Kelly Sherman; my father and stepmother, Gerald and Jael; all of you are showing how to make positive changes in Indian Country; my younger brothers and sisters, Ben, Luke, Sarabeth, and Bekkah; Charlene Hollow Horn Bear and her beautiful family; our uncles Marlon, Ben, and Richard Sherman; and Lori Pourier (First People's Fund).

Thank you to those who have helped bring our vision to these pages: Beth Dooley, writer, collaborator, and friend; photographers Nancy Bundt, Mette Nielsen, and Heidi Ehalt for capturing the spirit of our work; the University of Minnesota Press team, including Laura Westlund, David Thorstad, and especially our editor, Erik Anderson, who believed in us first.

Finally, my deepest thanks to Dana Thompson, business partner, fierce ally, apt critic, devout fan, and love of my life, and our beautiful, strong children Evie Odden and Phoenix Danger: may you help carry this precious world into the future.

THE SIOUX CHEF TEAM IS HONORED BY THE SUPPORT OF OUR KICKSTARTER COMMUNITY. YOU HELPED US MAKE REAL THE SHARED DREAM OF AN INDIGENOUS KITCHEN.

The 318 Cafe

Kyle Anderson

Lee E Anderson

Chris Anton

Mary Frances Arquette

Abdul-Elah Baghdadi

Moira Bateman

Mary Beeson

Suzanne Begin

Dr. Christopher A. Bergman

Black Sheep Cafe

Kathleen Brakke

Stephan H. Braun

Bob and Cathy Brill

David R. Brinkworth

Molly Broder

Li-Ming Chen

Sherri L. Cook

Cory Cornelius

Vanessa Dayton

Gabriel Dhahan

Stacey Diaz

Serge Dohmen and Jassir

Terry and Lea Dooley

Julie and Mike Druschke

Michelle Dziak

Adam Monier Edwards

Given in honor of Dr. James Ericson
(Stefani Conyers, Caitlin Knight,
Mallory Lauerhunt)

Jayne E. Ferguson

Clarissa D. Ford

Ivette and Austin Fragomen

Mariah Gladstone

Wendy Greenberg and Mark Fulton

Jan M. Haapala

Emelie Haigh

Larry and Mary Hall of the Flathead
Reservation

Greg Handberg

Dennis Hanold and Barb Kucera

Kaziah and Greg Haviland-Montgomery

Ellen Heck

Maureen Gaffney Henderson

James High

George Hirst

Fred Holzapfel

Linton Hopkins

Anil B. Hurkadli

Matt Hutson

Isaac

Erik Jensen

D. W. Johnson

Nancy Johnson, IWI's Seed Institute

Marilyn Dee Jones

Nina Reamer Jones

Don Kackman and Daisy Landvik

Donna Kamann and Eric Christensen

Robert Kellerman

Barbara Kenmille

Peter and Françoise Kirkpatrick

Patricia Klees

John Kohlsaat

Wendy Kvale

Melinda Ladd

Justin Lansing

Kayla L. Luft

Joan M Mailander, PHN

Laura McClusky

Devon Mihesuah

Catherine Miller and Tom McMasters

Eric and Elizabeth Miller

John Minutaglio, Pooja, Rohan, and Tian

Eric, Kate, and Eleanor Moran

Megumi Nakai

Monique Noel

J. Diane Oliver-Jensen

Emma O'Polka

Mason F. Pacini

Jennifer and Davin Peelle

Chris and Seth Peter

Pam and Matt Peterson

Mark Pizarek

John Polivick

Bryan Pollard

Jed Portman

Cindi Ptak

Lakota Quanah

Kevin Rappana

Amy Reams

Madeleine Rex

Arthur C. Robb

John W. Robinson

Russell J. Brent Roque

Victoria Rosario

Steve and Kris Rose

Laura Mitchell Ross and John Walker Ross

Geneo J. Samuel

The Sandoval Family

Cedar Schimke

Kristina A. Schlecht

Beatrice S. Schneider, Chicago Culinary FX

Charlie Schneider, Morgon Mae Schultz, and Patrick Schilling

Allison Schwarz

Claudia Serrato

Jason and Stevie Shea

Ben Sherman

Gerald Sherman

Jonathan Kyle Slater

Ted and Kim Smith

David Souther and Annie Levine

Stuart Stanley

Heidi and Judy Steltzner

Karen Stoker

Melissa Stuke

Adrian Swartout

Stefanie Teggemann

Alicia Thomas

Jennifer Thompson and Christopher Stevens

Molly Tindle

Lissa Treiman

Corinna Vigier

StarFyre Pabani Waban

Susan Weiner

Matthew A. Weir

Gwen Westerman and Glenn Wasicuna

Kachina Yeager

Pat and Steph Yoon

maryam marne zafar

Patina Park Zink

RESOURCES

As Sean continues to collect resources, he will update
the Sioux Chef Web site (www.sioux-chef.com).

Abbott, Patrick J. "American Indian and Alaska Native Aboriginal Use of Alcohol in the United States." *American Indian and Alaska Native Mental Health Research* 7(2): 1–13.

Albala, Ken. *Food Cultures of the World Encyclopedia,* Vol. 2. Santa Barbara, Calif.: Greenwood, 2011.

Baudar, Pascal. *The New Wildcrafted Cuisine: Exploring the Exotic Gastronomy of Local Terroir.* White River Junction, Vt.: Chelsea Green Publishing, 2016.

Cox, Beverly, and Martin Jacobs. *Spirit of the Harvest: North American Indian Cooking.* New York: Stewart, Tabori and Chang, 1991.

Divina, Fernando, Marlene Divina, and the Smithsonian National Museum of the American Indian. *Foods of the Americas: Native Recipes and Traditions.* Berkeley: Ten Speed Press, 2004.

Frank, Lois Ellen. *Foods of the Southwest Indian Nations: Traditional and Contemporary Native American Recipes.* Berkeley: Ten Speed Press, 2002.

Geniusz, Mary Siisip, and Wendy Makoons Geniusz. *Plants Have So Much to Give Us, All We Have to Do Is Ask: Anishinaabe Botanical Teachings.* Minneapolis: University of Minnesota Press, 2015.

Hetzler, Richard. *The Mitsitam Café Cookbook: Recipes from the Smithsonian National Museum of the American Indian.* Golden, Colo.: Fulcrum Publishing, 2010.

Kavasch, E. Barrie. *Native Harvests: American Indian Wild Foods and Recipes.* Mineola, N.Y.: Dover Publications, 1977.

Kimmerer, Robin Wall. *Braiding Sweetgrass: Indigenous Wisdom, Scientific Knowledge, and the Teachings of Plants.* Minneapolis: Milkweed Editions, 2013.

Kuhnlein, Harriet V., and Nancy J. Turner. *Traditional Plant Foods of Canadian Indigenous Peoples: Nutrition, Botany and Use.* Phildelphia: Gordon and Breach Publishers, 1991.

Marshall, Joseph M., III. *The Journey of Crazy Horse: A Lakota History.* New York: Penguin, 2004.

———. *The Lakota Way: Stories and Lessons for Living.* New York: Penguin, 2001.

Miller, Jen. "Frybread: This Seemingly Simple Food Is a Complicated Symbol in Navajo Culture." Smithsonianmag.com/arts-culture/frybread-79191.

Moerman, Daniel E. *Native American Food Plants: An Ethnobotanical Dictionary.* Portland, Ore.: Timber Press, 2010.

Ross, Anne, Kathleen Pickering Sherman, Jeffrey G. Snodgrass, Henry D. Delcore, and Richard Sherman. *Indigenous Peoples and the Collaborative Stewardship of Nature: Knowledge Binds and Institutional Conflicts*. London: Routledge, 2011.

Segrest, Valerie, and Elise Krohn. *Feeding the People, Feeding the Spirit: Revitalizing Northwest Coastal Indian Food Culture*. Seattle: Chatwin Books, 2010.

Turner, Nancy J. *Ancient Pathways, Ancestral Knowledge: Ethnobotany and Ecological Wisdom of Indigenous Peoples of Northwestern North America*. Vancouver: University of British Columbia Press for the Royal British Columbia Museum, 1997.

Vennum, Thomas, Jr. *Wild Rice and the Ojibway People*. St. Paul: Minnesota Historical Society Press, 1988.

Wilson, Gilbert L. *Buffalo Bird Woman's Garden*. St. Paul: Minnesota Historical Society Press, 1987.

PHOTOGRAPHY CREDITS

David Bowman: page 82.

Philip Breker: page 13, page 19, page 27, page 67, page 78, page 94, page 94, page 100, page 111, page 119, page 118, page 147, page 164, page 181, page 181, page 181.

Nancy Bundt: page 6, page 45, page 50, page 54, pages 55–56, page 68, page 76, page 79, page 85, page 88, page 91, page 205, page 115, page 116, page 120, page 132, page 135, page 139, page 152, page 160, page 171, page 173, page 172, page 174, page 176, page 178, page 183, page 226.

Heidi Ehalt: page 134, page 173, page 181, page 182, page 183, page 196.

Elizabeth Hoover: page 12, page 16, page 48, page 49, page 80, page 184.

Eliesa Johnson for SeriousEats.com: page 122.

Minnesota Historical Society: page 34, photograph by Gilbert Livingstone Wilson, 42094; page 49, photograph by Carl Gustave Linde, 60674; page 80; page 179.

Mette Nielsen: page ii, page 14, page 21, page 22, page 30, page 39, page 42, page 58, page 61, page 62, page 72, page 84, page 90, page 95, page 112, page 114, page 124, page 127, page 137, page 154, page 157, page 161, page 162, page 167, page 177, page 180.

Sean Sherman: page 1, page 25, page 36, page 44, page 53, page 76, page 77, page 84.

Dana Thompson: page 33, page 75, page 71, page 104, page 117, page 148.

INDEX

SEAN SHERMAN (Oglala Lakota) is revitalizing indigenous cuisine. With his business partner Dana Thompson, he launched The Sioux Chef, a catering and educational enterprise based in the Twin Cities. The award-winning Sioux Chef Tatanka Truck features pre-Contact foods of the Dakota and Minnesota territories. The Sioux Chef has been featured in the *New York Times, Atlantic Monthly,* and on National Public Radio, as well as in local, national, and international publications. Sherman and his team share their vision through lectures and presentations, and and they have prepared dinners at the United Nations, Slow Foods Indigenous Terra Madre in India and Italy, and the James Beard House.

BETH DOOLEY is the author of several award-winning cookbooks, including *Savoring the Seasons of the Northern Heartland* (Minnesota, 2004), coauthored with Lucia Watson; *The Northern Heartland Kitchen* (Minnesota, 2011); *Minnesota's Bounty: The Farmers Market Cookbook* (Minnesota, 2013); and *Savory Sweet: Simple Preserves from a Northern Kitchen* (Minnesota, 2017), coauthored with Mette Nielsen. She has also written a memoir, *In Winter's Kitchen: Growing Roots and Breaking Bread in the Northern Heartland.*

NOTES

NOTES

NOTES

NOTES